MW00721556

BIRTH, DEATH, AND OTHER TRIVIALITIES

A Humorous Philosophical Look at the Human Condition

BIRTH, DEATH, AND OTHER TRIVIALITIES

A Humorous Philosophical Look at the Human Condition

MARCEL STRIGBERGER

Three Beans Press
San Ramon, California 94583

Although the author and publisher have made every effort to ensure the accuracy and completeness of information contained in this book, we assume no responsibility for errors, inaccuracies, omissions, or any inconsistency herein. Any slights of people, places, or organizations are unintentional.

"Chop Chop" (pages 127-31) was first published in *Lawyer's Weekly*. "The Dental Crusades" (pages 105-09) was first published in *Stitches, The Journal of Medical Humor*.

First printing 1997

ISBN 0-9653595-0-6

LCCN 96-61137

TABLE OF CONTENTS

CHAPTER ONE
BIRTH, DEATH, AND OTHER TRIVIALITIES   1

CHAPTER TWO
HAPPINESS IS . . .   23

CHAPTER THREE
MONEY, MONEY, MONEY   49

CHAPTER FOUR
WAR AND PEACE   65

CHAPTER FIVE
MD, PHD, AND OTHER D'S   87

CHAPTER SIX
BUT IS HE A REAL DENTIST?   103

CHAPTER SEVEN
LAW, NOT A NOTE THAT FOLLOWS SO   113

CHAPTER EIGHT
PEOPLE NEEDING PEOPLE   139

ACKNOWLEDGEMENT AND DEDICATION

The final chapter of this book suggests three reasons why people need other people. I did not require the following people for any of those reasons. But they were crucial in my drive and motivation in getting this book published.

Thank you do Barry Seltzer, eminent legal and artistic colleague for illuminating the road for me and encouraging me to publish my thoughts.

And thanks to Malcolm Lester, for your generous mentoring throughout. Like the caterpillar to Alice, you were always there to tell me where to go to from here.

I dedicate this opus to my dynamic wife Shoshana and to our offspring Danny, Natalie and Gabriel, whose frequent impossible behavior, which often was not funny while it was happening, inspired a number of the episodes in this book.

And to you dear reader, I am grateful for you taking the time to indulge on this humorous philosophical panorama of life. I guarantee this study of the human condition will be a lot more amusing than reading Sartre; and it won't be on the exam!

CHAPTER 1

BIRTH, DEATH, AND OTHER TRIVIALITIES

EXIT, STAGE UP

This is as good a time as any to discuss death.

Have you ever noticed that the English language has a myriad of expressions for this event, which rivals only taxes as being a certainty?

I recently met an insurance broker as I was in the market for life insurance. It's not that I expected imminently to *go*. It was simply just in case. I couldn't make up my mind there and then about the merits of his wares and I asked the man to call me back the following Tuesday. The broker responded, "What if *something should happen to you meanwhile?*" I didn't catch on.

I queried, "What might happen between Thursday and next Tuesday?" Offhand, the only plans I had entailing some risk was for a haircut on Friday.

The broker replied, "You never know, something might happen."

Since he was in the business of selling life insurance, I found it rather strange he wouldn't just come out and simply say, "You might *drop dead.*"

Put this way it probably would have made me think. Even if I would not have grabbed his life insurance policy that Thursday, at least I would have been extra careful. I probably would not have let my barber shave my throat.

Somehow the expression "something happens" doesn't sound as terminal as "death." Although I can live with that expression I simply cannot see the media using it to connote death. Imagine how readers would react if a newspaper obituary column carried the following listing: George Dingle, 73 years of age, at the Riverdale Hospital. Something happened to him.

I for one would be a bit concerned about poor George and rather curious as to what happened to him. Other readers might even call the hospital to see whether George was all right and to see whether they could help.

Now if, for example, the listing went on to describe where and when the funeral would take place, it would confirm our worst suspicions. We'd know for sure George was *no more.* Although if we were to call the funeral parlor and ask about George Dingle, they would just tell us Mr. Dingle is "resting" there.

This is a fair statement, I guess, as poor George would need all the rest he could get in view of the long trip ahead of him across the Stygian River to the next world, assuming, of course, there is life after something happens.

But there is also a myriad of similar expressions that make death sound less decisive or at least less final.

Sometimes a person is said to *expire*. Like a Visa card: Expires September 1998. This is not as bad as it sounds. Chances are you'll get a new card in the mail in August that will tie you over until September 1999. I would certainly choose expiry over death in the hope of ultimately having my stay on earth extended, even if only for one year at a time.

Most of the other expressions fall similarly into the category of words or phrases tending to show the deceased is *no longer with us*. We will hear that George Dingle (we may as well use George and not *waste* anybody else) has *passed on* or has *departed*. This trip may sometimes find George converted into a chattel as people might say they have *lost* George.

This latter term, however, connotes some measure of hope of recovery or return; as when something is lost, there is always the lost and found office. It may only be a small chance but a lost George is more likely to be found sitting among the purses and umbrellas than a *mortified* George; one who so to speak had *bit the dust*.

And speaking of chances, what happens to a man if his *number is up?* This term is ideal for lottery players and fatalists. He doesn't die; his number is just up. It's as if there's some angel of death in the netherworld turning a huge drum and pulling out people's social insurance numbers.

Children have no fear calling a spade a spade. Whenever they play military games, they have no hesitation to shout, "Bang, you're dead!" I used to play these games with my French-Canadian pals in my

3

hometown of Montreal; whenever I was mortally wounded in combat they'd usually shout, "Bang, bang, *tu est finis*."

They declared me to be finished, like a soft-boiled egg.

And once someone, say George again, does *pop off* (I can live with that one too), he is known as the *late* George. This expression, in my opinion, adds insult to injury, especially if ascribed to an individual who was usually punctual all his life. How could he possibly be on time now when he has no way of getting to where he's expected? Why call him late? It's not his fault he *kicked the bucket*.

There's absolutely no justification in calling the individual late once he's gone *belly up*. Late people still eventually do show up. But George isn't coming back unless he's got those strange powers Patrick Swayze had in the movie *Ghost*.

On the brighter side of things, at least there's overwhelming proof that there is life after death. If there wasn't, people would never go around saying George has *gone to meet his Maker*.

CAN ST. PETER COME OUT AND PLAY?

Personally, I believe we all go somewhere after that last curtain call. This is one of the reasons I try to be a good boy and I don't bother anybody much. There is no way, for example, I would go over to any man wearing a silly-looking hat, yank it off his head, and flip it away. I don't know about other people but the thought of having to account for it in the next world is somewhat of a deterrent for me.

When the angels take inventory of my sins and naughty acts, I don't want Gabriel or whoever looks after these things punching the keyboard and up comes . . . "Strigberger, Marcel . . . social insurance number #536-354-990, Toronto . . . flipped man's hat into the snow."

I just know someone up there takes stock of these things.

None of us knows what takes place for sure. Those of us who saw the movie *Ghost* have a leg up on most scholars of the subject. In that movie the hero's spirit hung around in this world after he got shot to death. For the duration of the film the hero influenced the course of events.

To a certain extent this sounds fair to me. It would be nice for people who were done in during the prime of their life to at least get to watch the show from wherever they are now and to get some satisfaction from their vindication.

Look at Mozart, for example. He died a pauper in his mid-thirties. Today he is revered as the greatest musical composer who ever lived. Wouldn't it be just right if he could observe what is happening and turn to Salieri and say, "See!"

Or Van Gogh. He couldn't sell more than one painting in his lifetime. It fetched him the grand total of one hundred dollars. (At least it was one hundred U.S. dollars as opposed to one hundred Canadian dollars.) Some of his paintings have been auctioned off in London's fancy houses during the past decade for fifty million dollars. It would only be just if old

Vincent could get some satisfaction out of the proceedings. Maybe he does. Who knows?

"Ladies and gentlemen we have a bid of 350,000 dollars for Van Gogh's *Sunflower*. Do I hear more? . . . Who said twenty million dollars? It sounded like it came from you, Mr. Suzuki . . . There, I hear that voice again, thirty million dollars? . . . It's not you, Mr. Suzuki? . . . Did you hear it too, Mrs. Suzuki? Now who said thirty-five million dollars? I definitely heard thirty-five, in a Dutch accent . . . from behind that floating catalog."

Still, no matter what, the money wouldn't go to Vincent. But the thought is nice.

ENTER, STAGE CENTER

I don't quite remember when I discovered how babies were born. I do know that it was a closely guarded secret among the European parents in my neighborhood, including my own. Whenever I would ask my mother she would always blush and say something like, "You'll find out when you grow up."

The thought of gaining this knowledge down the road was certainly an incentive for me to grow up.

But at that time it was easier to get the answer to the mystery of Stonehenge.

At one point I was convinced women developing a large belly had something to do with it. I recall having an international conference on this subject around the time I was in kindergarten with my pals on the street of my downtown Montreal neighborhood. The discussions were inconclusive, but Nicky Pappas, whose mother had recently come down with the fat-belly syndrome, said he would ask his mother about the phenomenon and report back to us.

The next day when the summit conference resumed we were none the wiser. Nicky said that his mother simply blushed. His dad meanwhile told him to go out and play hockey.

Jean Luc, one of ten children in his family, was not much help either. He had seen a correlation between his mother's inflated belly and a baby coming. But all he could say for sure was his mother would go to the hospital. Then she would return with a baby.

"Could it be," Domenic queried, "that babies are sold at hospitals? Maybe the mother's tummy has nothing to do with it."

We thought that was an interesting theory.

But then the question was, why does it take so long? Why couldn't the parents just go to the hospital and buy the kid pronto? And why didn't the mother come home from the hospital right away. We all knew she went off into the night, not to return for about a week. These questions baffled us.

As did the hospital bit.

Certainly in the 1950s in Montreal, kids were not allowed to visit anyone in a hospital. I remember when my younger cousin was born, my uncle and my dad took my other cousin and I to the hospital to pick up the new arrival. Before they went into the elevator, they told us to wait in the lobby. I asked my father when I could come up and he said, "When you grow up."

My uncle said *if* we stayed put in the lobby and behaved, they would return with a surprise. A half-hour later out they rolled together with my aunt, who was carrying a baby. My cousin and I winked at one another. We had no doubt babies came from hospitals. In retrospect, I wonder what would have happened had we not behaved. What would they have done? Left the baby behind?

But the big break through came later in the day when my cousin jumped on my aunt. She said, "Be careful, Michael. I just had a baby."

Eureka! There was some substance to the baby-in-the-tummy theory. I called for another international conference on where babies come from. Nicky said he'd try again to get confirmation from his dad about it. Jean Luc didn't believe it, but he said he'd keep a close eye on his mother the next time it happened. Domenic was spellbound.

But all hell broke loose when Viktor, my Ukrainian friend, went home and related the theory to his parents. His mother came over to interrogate me. Actually, she was out to get me to recant this outrageous theory in front of Viktor.

"Where baby come from?" she asked in her thick accent.

"The lady's tummy," I replied, proudly.

"No. They come from Sears," she said.

Although it was a tempting thought, I knew the Sears version was wrong. I had been up and down the escalator oodles of times, and I never saw babies on sale there. Furthermore, I thought, if her theory was correct, then where had Cain and Abel come from? Mail order? At the risk of being branded a heretic and getting excommunicated, I stuck to my guns.

Now I knew what Galileo felt like. I was very proud of my discovery.

On the other hand the escalator at Sears didn't go up to the seventh floor. For this you had to take the elevator. Just like at the hospital. Hmm.

I don't know what Viktor's parents told him that night, but for some time thereafter he had this great desire to visit department stores.

I soon realized my discovery about the origin of babies didn't answer one question: How do the babies get into the mother's stomach? Where would I get the answer? I wasn't going to ask Viktor's mom. My own parents were evasive. My mother said they just start growing there once the lady gets married. "How do they know when to start growing?" I queried.

"Gabriel the angel tells them," she said.

I didn't buy the angel bit. And Domenic, Jean Luc, and Nicky all agreed they had never seen a man with wings around their homes talking to their mother's belly. We all knew there was more to it than that.

Not too long afterwards, all sorts of weird theories started circulating on the street, including one about the father having something to do with babies being born. Although it gave us all a chuckle, none of the guys believed our fathers would ever want to do something like that!

And when we told Viktor, he said, "At Sears?"

RELIGIONS 'N US . . . A TRILOGY:

1) The boss's son

I was a tour guide for Gray Line Sightseeing in Montreal for six summers. Although I have forgotten much of my spiel over the past twenty years, one fact that remains firmly embedded in my mind is the commentary I used to make about the fact that there were "over 450 churches in Montreal, more than in Rome."

And it was Mark Twain who said, "In Montreal you could hardly throw a stone without breaking a church window."

There being no military conscription in Canada, you could walk the streets for weeks without coming across a soldier. But you would only have to step outside on a main street in order to run into a nun or a priest. This would raise the curiosity of a little Jewish boy.

My parents always warned me not to get too close to them because they might try to convert me. My mother told me these people weren't too crazy about us, as we had allegedly killed Jesus. When I queried who Jesus was, my mother pointed to a silver likeness of the bearded man who was firmly affixed to a large cross dangling on the robe of a passing priest.

I felt sorry for the little man with the beard. I then asked my mother whether indeed we were responsible for Jesus' predicament and she said, "They think so." Further investigation revealed that some people called Romans, who are no longer around, killed Christ. I asked my mother if we were Roman, and she said "No, we're Jewish." Pointing to the priest she said, "He's Roman Catholic."

"That makes him a Roman," I replied.

"Sort of," mom answered.

The shocker came when she told me Jesus had been Jewish. When I heard this, I couldn't for the life of me figure out why Romans would have it in for Jews for allegedly killing another Jew especially when the Romans themselves did it. In fact, I still can't figure that one out.

2) *The boss's people*

I remember one day when I was six or seven years old my mother ran with me toward a streetcar stop on a blustery Montreal morning. We had almost made it to the step when the streetcar operator decided to take advantage of the green traffic signal and leave my mother and I to wait in the wind and frost for the next car.

In Yiddish, my mother shouted to the fugitive streetcar, "Anti-Semite!"

This was the first time I had heard this word. I asked her what it meant, and she told me the driver wouldn't wait for us as he was an anti-Semite. I didn't press her and she didn't go into details.

For the next while or so I lived with this idea of anti-Semitism. One day I was playing street hockey with my pal Viktor, when we noticed his mother running to catch a streetcar at the same stop. To her displeasure, the driver took off just before she made it to the door. Just out of earshot, she shouted something to the operator in Ukrainian that was curt and not too complimentary. I told Viktor she was calling the driver an anti-Semite. I explained that anti-Semites

11

were streetcar drivers who didn't wait for people who are running to the stop trying to catch them.

It was not too long before this new word was disseminated throughout the street. In due course, Viktor and I had the occasion to teach the word to our friends Nicky, Domenic, Sacha, Jean Luc, and his five brothers as we noticed a streetcar driver leaving behind a group of angry would-be passengers.

It got to the point that we would all shout loudly, "anti-Semite!" at the offending streetcar to the bewilderment of passengers and would be passengers. This became even more fun than throwing snowballs at the streetcar.

Anti-Semitism was rampant in the area. Hardly a day went by without a number of streetcars shooting through the intersection and leaving a handful of disgruntled people waving their hands and cursing.

One day the meaning of my newly learned and probably the longest word in my vocabulary took on a new twist. My father and I were watching a televised hockey game in the days when there were no such things as atheists or agnostics. Everyone knew of the existence of Montreal Canadians' superstar, Rocket Richard. And whenever the Rocket skated onto the ice there was hardly a kid in Montreal watching and wearing his red, white, and blue sweater who did not bow down three times in the direction of the Montreal Forum.

During one game after the Rocket scored yet another goal against Gordie Howe's Detroit Red Wings, my father waited until I took my lips off the screen and asked, "Why do you cheer for the Rocket so much? He's probably an anti-Semite."

I was shocked. What my dad said made no sense whatsoever. I asked myself, "Could it be the Rocket drives a streetcar during the summer season?"

But even if he did there was no way he could have been an anti-Semite. I just couldn't imagine his streetcar driving through the intersection of Saint Laurent and Saint Joseph Street, leaving a cluster of angry passengers marooned. Maybe Gordie Howe might do it. But not the Rocket.

Then again even if he did, he was the great Maurice the Rocket Richard and I wanted to grow up and follow in his skate steps. If he felt like making the green light and being an anti-Semite, so be it. He was still my hero.

I do not recall too much more about that evening except my father shutting the television set off in anger before the game was over. I couldn't figure out why as the Canadians were winning and the Rocket had just scored another goal. And all I said was when I grow up I wanted to be an anti-Semite.

I learned it was tough growing up a hockey fan with a streetcar on my street.

3) The boss

I don't remember at what age I first became aware of the concept of an infinite being. At one point or other my parents told me there was a God who knew all our thoughts and who held us accountable for all our actions. They would look up and point to the sky when the subject came up.

Naturally, I related this information to my good pal, Viktor. I told him about the man in the sky and what the man in the sky was capable of doing. I also related my newly acquired knowledge about life after death, namely that if you were good you went up to the sky where things were fun.

Initially, Viktor was skeptical, to say the least. He said, "Hi, man in the sky. Can you hear me?" This was followed by an assortment of gestures, but using different fingers than my parents would use.

I was petrified. I felt like the kid was playing Frisbee with a bottle of nitroglycerine. I said, "Viktor, stop that. He sees everything. You'll get us both into trouble."

This was definitely worse than getting a detention I thought.

I was also embarrassed. I was thinking to myself, "Dear man in the sky, I have nothing to do with Viktor. I'm out of here."

I was amazed nothing happened to him. No lightning bolt, nothing. Moreover, that afternoon we had been flipping for hockey cards and he cleaned me out with the best run of luck he had ever had. This got me on the hotline to the man in the sky.

"I don't understand it, God. I didn't make fun of you. Viktor did. So why did you punish me causing me to lose about thirty hockey cards? I even lost Rocket Richard. It's not fair."

You know what? I didn't get an answer. When I related the events of the afternoon to my mother, she responded very philosophically, "I told you before not to flip for hockey cards." This made me feel even worse. I felt abandoned not only by the man upstairs but also by my mother down here.

The next day Viktor told me he had spoken to his mom and she told him there is no such thing as a man in the sky. He felt his behavior the previous day was vindicated. He did, however, relate to me the bit about the importance of Jesus, naming me as one of the people responsible for his untimely departure. We had a fervent debate, each of us citing chapter and verse in support of our arguments, the highest of authorities, our respective mothers. The business about the Romans doing it fell on deaf ears.

Furthermore, he even denied Christ was Jewish to start with. He said, "If Jesus was Jewish, why would Ukrainians like him?"

I replied. "I don't know. I know that he was Jewish and we don't care for him."

The debate ended with neither of us scoring any points. Before Viktor went home he asked, "Do you want to flip more hockey cards?"

I'LL PRAY FOR YOU

There I was in my mid-teens at a French Catholic high school in Quebec City. It was strictly pleasure, not business. I was about to engage my opponent in the provincial high school team chess championship. Every room of the three-hundred-year-old cavernous seminary had a huge crucifix bearing a statue of Christ affixed to it hanging on the wall. It was the first time I had played a chess tournament match in this type of environment.

As was my custom and still is, I offer up a special silent prayer for the occasion hoping it all goes right.

It felt strange doing it with Jesus Christ looking down on me with his soft and somber eyes. I knew the purpose for having the cross in the room was no doubt to afford some type of protection. I had no problem with that but where did it place me?

It was a high-pressure game for both of us and my opponent was fidgeting incessantly. Along came his team coach, a priest. Looking at both of us, brother François said to Jean- Marc Leblanc, "I'll pray for you."

This comment had me thinking. I cried foul. Initially, I felt uneasy with Jesus staring at me. Now brother François was getting into gear against me. I wondered what kind of prayer he would say. Was he asking God to confound my thinking? Was he saying something like, "Dear Lord, let Strigberger forget to protect his knight?"

I studied the board, staring at my two bishops. The deck appeared more stacked against me now. Then again what should they have called those two slender cylindrical pieces on the board, rabbis? It then occurred to me that just minutes earlier I myself had offered up a prayer to the man in the sky asking that the game go right for me. Presumably, I got my foot through the door upstairs first. Brother François only got to rebut. In addition, I felt God owed me one. After all it was only fair I win this one, as that day in Montreal ten years earlier he let Viktor clean out my hockey cards. Finally, I looked at Jesus himself. I figured he and I were the only two Jews in the room. Maybe I would get some professional courtesy.

Three hours later the game ended in a draw. I never did figure out what went on upstairs. Would the result have been the same had none of us prayed?

Who knows? Maybe the outcome of the match was predetermined or predestined in any event. Perhaps years earlier there was a note in that great book upstairs that on April 21, 1964, the game between Jean-Marc and Marcel would end in a tie.

But I was not one to ever take unnecessary chances. Prayer is a crucial element in my life. And as Bob Hope once quipped while hosting yet another Oscar award event, "On Oscar night there are no atheists."

DO YOU BELIEVE?

Yes.

But I've always wondered about the atheist and the agnostic.

Where does the atheist get off being certain there is no man in the sky? How can you prove something does not exist? Has anyone ever proven UFOs don't exist. I don't believe they do, but I could never say with conviction they don't. Who can?

Or who can say the Loch Ness monster doesn't exist. Sightings have been reported over the years and until such time as the loch is fully explored, the mystery will remain.

With the concept of a Supreme Being the stakes are much higher. You see, if we believe and we draw a blank later on, big deal. Then we have gone through life in a world operating on automatic pilot. The four seasons, the ability of all animals to adapt to the environment to sustain themselves, and the wonder of the human heart which takes a licking but still keeps on ticking are all a big fluke. Right.

On the other hand if we don't believe, then the atheists could be in trouble down the road if indeed there is someone up there who set the whole business into motion and who watches over us—and over our hockey cards. They may not be in a pickle but they could be. They just may face a day of judgment after their demise where their maker or one of his agents (if that's the way it happens) says, "You blew it, Charlie. If you felt uncomfortable that day in July when the office air-conditioning broke down, wait until you go through door number two."

Fanatics on either side concern me. Give me a practical person anytime. I'll go on believing in the existence of the man in the sky and in studying the Old Testament until such time as Charles Darwin comes back for a visit and says, "Hey guys, it's okay."

THE GOOD BOOK . . .
"AND THEN HE CREATED LAUGHTER"

I have read the Old Testament over and over again and one thing perturbs me: Nobody has a sense of humor. The vignettes are colorful but they are all covered by an air of solemnity and harshness. The characters step out of line *once* and they get zapped.

Adam and Eve nibble on the forbidden fruit and what happens? They are banished from Eden and made to earn a living like the rest of us. No second chance. I would have been happier had God given them a warning: "Don't do it again or you can start looking for fig leaves."

Cain and Abel come into the picture and we see man's first homicide. Had Cain been endowed with a sense of humor he may have joked about the fact

Abel had continuous successes at the sacrificial altar while all of his own attempts resulted in lemons. Cain could have said something like, "I don't get no respect."

Cain's reaction however may have been the same had Abel done the joking, ribbing Cain as to why his own sacrifices were accepted while Cain's bombed. If it were my own little brother laughing at my altars, I'd garrote him.

And what happens when mankind is devoid of humor? A flood of course.

With Noah and his family spending days looking for a male and female of each species, surely there had to be at least one kibitzer.

Maybe there was; perhaps Ham, son number two. Perhaps he came up with zingers every day. Is it possible that as his father and two brothers were busy trying to determine whether a skunk was a male or a female, Ham stood by idly quipping, "Did you hear the one about the elephant and the flea?" Maybe this is the origin of the verb "ham." I only speculate.

The epitome of biblical severity is the story of the unfortunate wife of Lot. While the angels were busy barbecuing the cities of Sodom and Gomorrah, Mrs. Lot while fleeing defied a proscription not to look back; whereupon she immediately become a pillar of salt. I feel the punishment was rather harsh considering she was a first offender. After all, it's not as if she was notorious for being the peeping Tom of Goshen. Nor was the penalty itself published in advance. The angels never said, "Look back and you're salt." Being a lawyer, zero tolerance laws scare me.

One thing is for sure; this incident must have put the fear of the Lord into Lot. If he ever had any plans of buying some idols, he probably canceled his order promptly.

The Book of Exodus similarly isn't exactly Monty Python's Flying Circus. For starters, 450 years of Jewish slavery under the hands of the harsh Egyptian pharaohs is not funny. This is more so if the pharaohs even remotely resembled Yul Brynner.

Eventually, Moses comes into the picture, but the poor slaves have to wait an additional eighty years until Moses gets his calling as liberator. Until then all he does is beat up on evil Egyptian taskmasters and say, "Who me?"

And if misery is supposed to spawn humor, the theory remains unproven as there is no record of any Jewish slaves doing slavery comedy. There has to be something comical about building pyramids, but the Jews didn't hit it. Instead they frequently vented their frustrations by shouting at Moses, "Stone him, stone him!"

They don't even kid around when the plagues start hitting the Egyptians. I am not aware of any ancient Hebrew newsletter with stories entitled, *Now It's Boils.*

And what about the Jews at the Red Sea? What do they say to Moses as he's busy stroking his beard and trying to figure out how to get them across safely in the absence of a bridge which at this point would have been most useful? They shout, "Stone him, stone him!"

About the only thing humorous in Exodus up to this point is the word "smite." It just has to be the funniest word in the Bible, even funnier than "begat."

It appears man's sense of humor was in its cave-man state in biblical days, although heaven knows the pressures of the times warranted the luxury of a comical release. Perhaps if the Almighty were to amend the legislation today, there would be an eleventh commandment reading, "Thou shalt lighten up a little." But then again we must remember the real boss is God, not George Burns.

CHAPTER TWO

HAPPINESS IS . . .

IF YOU'RE HAPPY
AND YOU KNOW IT . . .

General James Wolfe of the British Army lay mortally wounded that fateful day in 1759 on the Plains of Abraham in Quebec City after the brief battle that resulted in the British wresting French Canada from France. As Wolfe was about to draw his last breath, he asked his assistant about the outcome of the battle. When told that he had been victorious, he said, "I die happy."

When I was studying ancient Greek history back in high school, our teacher told us the story of a Spartan woman who eagerly awaited news of the outcome of a battle the Spartans had been engaged in against the Persians and in which several of her sons were warriors. The messenger arrived and said something to the effect of, "Lady, I have bad news and good news. The bad news is four of your sons fell in the battle."

The woman then said, "That's not what I want to know. Did we win or lose the battle?"

When the Spartan messenger told her the Spartans had won, she said, "Excellent. Now let us celebrate."

Which brings me to Fort Lauderdale.

A couple of winters ago I was en route with my wife and three kids to the Fort Lauderdale airport headed back to Toronto after spending a few winter days in Florida hiding from our home cooked winters. My daughter Natalie, then thirteen years old—four years younger than number-one son Danny and four years older than number-two son Gabriel— allegedly had a miserable time in Florida. She was forced to spend her days lounging around by the hotel's swimming pool. She was abused by being taken on shopping sprees by her mother. And she was harassed and assaulted by being dragged to Florida attractions like Ocean World or Parrot Jungle and the like. She claimed she had never had a more miserable time in her life.

Heading for the airport both my sons were hung up on getting window seats on the plane. Natalie was prepared to take or leave a window seat. Her brothers each wanted one desperately and we were only being assigned two window seats on the flight. It would have been too simple for her to let each of the boys occupy this prime space.

And that's probably the very reason she threw her hat into the ring, also demanding a window seat, forcing me to draw lots to decide who would be the odd kid out.

As fate would have it she readily won the first coveted seat. The second prize went to number-one son

Danny leaving Gabriel kicking and screaming that life was no fair.

Gabriel, by the way, had enjoyed his time in Florida immensely. We couldn't get him out of the pool. He spent each morning looking forward to the events of the day and each evening being grateful to us for this lovely trip. But at this moment en route to the airport along Interstate 95, while I was cruising at 65 miles per hour trying to get to the airport in time, he was throwing a tantrum. The mother of all tantrums I would say.

Natalie's face suddenly lit up. An aura seemed to surround her doll-like features. She started to giggle. It was the first sign of laughter she had displayed since we made the initial announcement several weeks earlier that we would be going to Florida. She said softly, "I'm enjoying this. I leave Florida happy."

What the devil was she talking about? I asked myself. For almost two weeks my wife and I had showered the kid with attractions and activities, and she was miserable the moment we would say "no" to anything else she wanted. Now suddenly she was sincerely happy because her kid brother was not getting a window seat on the airplane?

Had I known what made her so happy I could have gone even further. I could have asked the airline to give Gabriel the lousiest seat on the plane. And no meals. Or perhaps I could have said to Gabriel, "Your sister is down a bit. I want you to walk to the airport."

Why didn't she tell me all along what made her happy?

I thought about Wolfe and that Spartan lady and about their respective ideas of absolute bliss. I then matched them next to Natalie's rapture and I started thinking.

WHAT IS IT?

I tried to figure out what happiness was all about. I found the results of these thoughts perplexing.

Take old General Wolfe for instance. Actually he wasn't old. He was all of thirty-two when he bit the dust (or if you sell insurance, when "something happened to him"). Was he really dying happy or was he just giving his listeners a line, something so outrageous that it would assure him a certain measure of fame? I mean, who would really have remembered had he said something like, "This is awful gentlemen. I could have returned to England a hero, decorated with all the medals His Royal Highness King George could pin on my chest. All the women in the Royal Court would be mine. Instead I'm afraid it's curtain time for me here in Quebec. It's a bloomin' pity."

In my opinion these words would not have been as memorable and as forceful a spokesman for the general's reputation. Nobody in fact knows what his adversary French General Montcalm said before he went on to meet his maker. The reason for this is probably because being French he was a trifle more emotional and upset after buying a musket ball or two. He probably just said something like, "*Merde, I'm hit.*" Short and to the point.

And what about that Spartan lady? I have heard different versions of that story since my high school days. The versions actually differ only as to the number of sons who fell. Could she really have been in the mood to celebrate under the circumstances? One would expect that a loss of a couple of sons or even one son might dampen her spirits.

But then again we must remember that the Spartans were Spartans. They lived a Spartan life. They never did anything lavishly, being content to keep it meager and simple. A Spartan couple wouldn't overindulge their kids by taking them on fancy vacations to the Riviera or by moving into palatial quarters. Papa Spartan would probably just have said, "I don't care what the guys up in Athens are doing. We don't need a roof."

I don't propose to preach as to how happiness can be achieved. I do propose to talk on what perplexes me about the way some people can be unhappy when they apparently have it all, yet others can be blissful when, in the words of cartoon character Foghorn Leghorn, "Ah say, it don't look so good."

GETTING IT

I imagine one thing that brings on a feeling of happiness is getting what you are shooting for and arriving where it is you are heading.

An almost universal goal of kids is to be able to drive their parent's car. I say almost universal as some parents like my own never owned a vehicle, and accordingly I never had the urge to bug my father for the car.

I did bother him frequently to buy one (so that I could get to drive it in the near future), but his excuse was he was afraid to drive. He said he would consider getting a car if there were fewer drivers on the road. I never accepted his excuse of fear of other drivers. To this day I feel the reason for my father not driving was some compelling feeling on the inside. I believe his body was possessed by the soul of an Amish.

He always told me that one day, when I grew up I could drive. At age eighteen I obtained my driver's license. I didn't get my first car until I turned twenty-seven, also being the very month Danny was born. Indeed, during the nine-year gap having the license per se was not too great a thrill.

And ever since Danny could talk he had been after me to let him drive the car. He would sit in my lap and with his growing hands firmly on the steering wheel he would tell me that this was paradise. The ecstasy known only by those who have not sinned after they enter the netherworld. There was no greater pleasure even approaching this experience. Although tempted, I wasn't going to engage him in a debate on this one. When he hit his teen years I let him drive a bit in abandoned parking lots to allow him relieve his urge.

I always said to him, "Danny, you'll get over the thrill after driving for four weeks."

"No dad, never, never, never. I love it, I love it," he would retort.

As he approached sixteen years of age, on the verge of getting a license, his enthusiasm was still that of a puppy who had just discovered the land of Alpo. I said to him,

"Danny, you'll be driving the car soon. There will come times where we may ask you to drive Natalie or Gabriel somewhere. Or we may send you to the supermarket or on some other chore, day or night. Will you be as enthusiastic to drive then as you have been all these times in the parking lots?"

"Knock it off dad," he would respond. How could I even suggest for a moment that for the rest of his life he might ever refuse the opportunity to drive a car?

My suspicions about his vim and vigor ever waning were wrong. His enthusiasm didn't last four weeks; it lasted about eight weeks. There was no problem initially getting him to help with the supermarket trips and the occasional car pool. My wife and I couldn't believe how we had lucked out. After sixteen years, number one son was finally of some measurable utility to us. We felt we had acquired a genie.

After a couple of months we started to notice gradual and subtle changes in Danny's attitude. One evening we asked him to go to the store to buy some tomato paste in order for us to cook my favorite spaghetti dinner. Danny, never one to be at loss whenever he wants to get out of doing something said "You can make spaghetti sauce without tomato paste."

I agreed that although in theory this form of culinary expression had some merit, my favorite spaghetti dish which we had been cooking for twenty years called for tomato paste. After listening to the kid's pleading for two minutes I told him there was no way we were going to substitute ketchup for tomato paste. I added that if I wanted further advice on how to cook I would consult Julia Child.

He conceded and grudgingly drove to the store.

A couple of months later I asked him to pick his sister up from a friend's house located all of a half mile from our house.

He went for my jugular. He said, "I'd love to dad, but I have homework to do. I have a geography test next week. You don't want me to fail do you?"

The genie had gone back to the bottle. I decided to pick up Natalie myself.

On the way home Natalie said to me, "Oh, it must be so much fun to drive a car. Can you teach me?"

I said to her, "Do you know the ingredients of spaghetti sauce?"

She hasn't asked for the car again.

NOT GETTING IT

You can, therefore, attain happiness when you get what you want, namely the chance to drive a car. A similar level of happiness awaits you when you get rid of something you do not want, say a volley of pain.

During my university student days, the worst time of the year was April. Exams exerted immense pressure on me. In addition, I always seemed to be in love at that time of year, having just fallen in love weeks earlier with some girl who had other matters than my serenades on her mind and who couldn't care less about the flowers that bloom in the spring.

My number one dream at the time was to simply get through the next set of exams. I knew once May arrived I would be in absolute ecstasy, no problem.

I would write the exams, usually do well, May would roll in and I would almost hear this lovely spring month talking to me.

The conversation would go something like this:

"So Marcel, my sister April is gone. The wicked exams are over. Aren't you glad to see me?"

Although I'd feel great the day of the final exam at the end of April, a day or two later I'd find myself totally let down and depressed for some inexplicable reason. There I was, four months ahead of me without the luxury of academic pressures. Surely there had to be more to life. I even had time to devote myself full time to pursuing this year's Miss April. But it wasn't the same without the additional pressures of a full slate of exams on my plate.

I imagine Mother Nature simply brought her into my life every year at that time in order to help dilute the intense focus I had on my exams. I was now thus given a headache to take my mind off the sore thumb.

The goal of finishing exams was attained and happiness arrived with it, but as is often the case, it lasted the life span of a butterfly.

SOME FOR ME PLEASE

It's hard for each of us to understand why the person who has achieved goals we may never attain in our lifetimes wouldn't be in an absolute state of ecstasy.

As a child growing up in Montreal I was a devoted Montreal Canadians hockey fan. My fantasy was to get to see a game live at the Montreal Forum. It was generally impossible to obtain a seat, a situation that hasn't changed much in thirty-five years. (Actually that's not totally true. When the Forum was mothballed in March of 1996, they were selling the seats as souvenirs. But that's not exactly what I envisaged!)

One day my father surprised me by bringing home two tickets to a game against the Detroit Red Wings. But the tickets were not for seats. They were for the privilege of standing for two to three hours four-deep behind the gray seats. From that height I could have gotten a better view had I watched the game from aboard the Goodyear Blimp. But I was thrilled to go, thrilled to breath the same air as Rocket Richard and Gordie Howe, albeit only for a couple of hours.

As I was watching a period (from atop of my father's shoulders), Gordie Howe drew a minor penalty. He was furious with the referee. He slammed his stick to the ice and he uttered some expletives even I was able to lip read from my distance. I couldn't figure out what the problem was. I felt like shouting, "Gordie, why are you angry? At least you're getting to see this game free."

This star was the idol of thousands of fans. Kids would sell their mothers to get his hockey card. He was famous and rich, earning probably more than thirty thousand dollars per year in the mid-1950s. This is probably less than Wayne Gretzky earns per game today, but it was nothing to sneeze at considering the average wage earner then pulled in about sixty dollars per week.

I told my father had I been in Gordie Howe's skates, there is no way I would have thrown that tantrum just for getting a two-minute penalty. I would simply have said to myself, "Hey, I'm the great Gordie Howe. I make more money than any of the fifteen thousand people sitting here tonight. What's a two-minute penalty in my great life? Show me the way to the box."

Maybe it is a question of degree. I've never noticed Gretzky or Eric Lindross getting a penalty, but maybe when they do, they simply focus on the fact they pull in a seven-figure income per year and laugh the whole thing off. Other players who earn, say, only five hundred thousand, probably consider themselves in a different league and have good reasons to be miserable. So they kick and scream whenever the ref blows the whistle and sends them to the sin bin.

Perhaps there is a cut-off line somewhere. You make over five hundred thousand dollars per year and you get a penalty, you're calm. You take it in stride. Four hundred thousand to a half million is a gray area. You fret and fume only if you get a major or maybe a totally unjustified minor penalty. If you earn under four hundred thousand dollars and you get a penalty, you can be Attila the Hun himself. You don't have to put up with this insult and abuse for a measly couple of hundred thousand per year.

SMILE, YOU'RE NOT ON CANDID CAMERA

But haven't we all noticed how glum and depressed the players on a losing team appear at the end of that final Stanley Cup match. As they move along the receiving line shaking hands with the victors their heads are pointing south and the expressions on their faces rival the look of Marie Antoinette as she was about to keep her date with Madame Guillotine.

Here are twenty professional hockey players who, by virtue of making it into the finals, have picked up bonus money exceeding what many people earn a whole year. They have participated in making hockey history in the world's most prestigious league, and yet there is not a smile on any face.

Whoever said, "It's not whether you win or lose, but how you play the game"? Whoever it was obviously never played the game. He probably just watched it, from the top of his father's shoulders, behind the gray seats in the Montreal Forum.

MODIFIED RAPTURE

Even the great Napoleon Bonaparte was miserable most of his life. He reputedly said that he did not enjoy "six days of happiness."

Here is a man who did have it all, except Russia I guess. And perhaps the height of Michael Jordan. But he still could have had enough fun with the rest of the world.

The guy owned all of France. Imagine what you could do with that.

A few years ago I visited Paris, and the doorman at Maxim's restaurant wouldn't let me in to take a peek because I was wearing shorts. Napoleon would not have suffered this disgrace. I'm sure the doorman would have overlooked the emperor's shorts. Or should I say the short emperor's shorts.

I have my greatest laugh whenever I read King Solomon's lamentation in Ecclesiastes, wherein His Highness in discussing material acquisitions and happiness says: "Everything is vanity." This man was probably the richest king in his time. He also had one thousand wives. I have never even counted to one thousand.

I don't know where Solomon gets off telling us "everything is vanity" and expecting us to believe it unless we've tried it ourselves. I myself am happily married (with one wife), but if I would be in a position to accurately test the king's proposition, no doubt I would have to have at least a random sampling of maybe ten or twenty wives before I could conclude that, yes indeed, it's not all it's made out to be.

And I am certain the wise king never had problems like I did with women in April. I have read Ecclesiastes several times and I still have not found out how Solomon did it.

I don't think if I were in Solomon's sandals that I ever would have made a comment like he did about it all being vanity. I know I probably would have said something like, "It could be demanding but it's got its good days."

The king's wisdom doesn't stop there. He goes on to say that in order to cheer yourself up and get a perspective on your life, you should remind yourself, "This too shall pass."

This is supposed to be comforting for the person who has zip while the next guy has an abundance of everything good.

Actually, it is a noble thought. Yet I would have loved to see Solomon telling this with three or four women by his side to the poor bugger who was still doing the singles scene in the inns of downtown Jerusalem.

"Don't worry son. Be happy. There's more to life than having your love life being four aces. This too shall pass."

It's a wonder the wise king had time to sort out babies between the feuding mothers.

HOW LOW CAN YOU GO?

On the other hand there may be some solace in that phrase to the person who is in the doldrums and who can only go up. But is there really such a place as bottom? I don't think so. Whenever one thinks he or she has hit the skids it is amazing how many times one can discover yet a lower level.

In grade nine after a difficult algebra exam, a few of us decided to pull a gag on a classmate Ronnie Shapiro. Shapiro was a wiz at history and English literature, but he was hopeless in math. He simply had a mental block when dealing with numbers and as a result failed virtually every math test he took. It was so bad the teacher would simply ask, "Shapiro, a train leaves Windsor Station in Montreal traveling sixty miles per hour . . ."

Shapiro would say, "I know there's going to be another train leaving New York City at some ridiculous speed soon, Mr. McBride, but why in the world should we care when the two trains will meet?"

But ask him to give you the history of the royal Windsor family and he could spew it out like an encyclopedia. Then again I would ask, who cares about the history of the royal Windsor family?

Unfortunately for Shapiro, the algebra exam focused more on speeding trains meeting somewhere near Albany, New York than it did on the Windsor clan. The fateful day arrived when Mr. McBride brought in the marked papers and started handing them out.

I don't know what they do these days in high schools but the custom then was for the teacher to engage in the degrading and terrifying practice of calling out the mark of each student. And for the embarrassment it caused to some of those victims their grades may as well have been published in *Newsweek*.

Before the algebra period a few of us decided to play a ruse on Shapiro by spreading a rumor that we had a peek at his paper and his grade was forty-seven, three shy of a passing mark.

For what it's worth, the ruse wasn't my idea. It was started by a couple of the guys who did lousy in history. Of course.

When the rumor reached Shapiro's ears he was visibly shaken. After seeing the poor bugger stew a short while I had sympathy on him and said, "Ronnie, it was just a joke. None of us saw your paper. You don't have forty-seven."

With that comment Ronnie Shapiro's mood did a 180-degree turn (I don't believe Shapiro would have understood this metaphor). He was suddenly the happiest kid in the class, chirping like a sparrow.

The rest of us meanwhile sat in the classroom in trepidation waiting for Mr. McBride to enter the classroom and start the slaughter. Except for Shapiro, we were all about as at ease as those members of the Bugsy Moran gang in that Chicago warehouse on St. Valentine's Day in 1929. In fact, those seven gangsters were better off; they were put out of their misery quicker.

The teacher entered and handed out the papers one by one calling out the names and the grades of each. They were in no particular order and about halfway down, he said, "Ronnie Shapiro: 43."

Poor Shapiro was besides himself. His face turned a neat shade of snow white. I had to run out of the classroom as I couldn't control my side-splitting laughter.

I did mean well when I told him minutes earlier 47 was not his real grade. But I didn't expect this. It seems there is always room to slip a little further.

Ronnie Shapiro eventually surprised us all and somehow made it into medical school and became a doctor. I presume even if he somehow overcame his number deficiency, his ever-sharp mind for historical facts is still his hallmark, and he will forever remember the algebra exam incident. I am certain the nightmare of any of his former classmates is to find ourselves pants dropped in front of Dr. Shapiro and the good doctor says, "Cough."

LOSING IT

Just like getting it, losing it can also make you happy. That is, once you get it back.

There is the joke about the guy who returns home from Las Vegas and his friend asks him how he did. He replies: "Great! I broke even, and boy did I need the money."

I imagine this surge of happiness is based on some principal that we probably don't know how good we have it until something of value is removed from us.

In the *Wizard of Oz,* for example, Dorothy is upset at Auntie Emm and Uncle Henry for not going to the wall for her when Myra Gulch comes to their home to remove Dorothy's little dog Toto. This is after the local sheriff, at the insistence of Ms. Gulch, has declared the little dog a menace to the community.

Dorothy runs off from home and eventually ends up in Oz.

She returns home to Kansas only by the grace of Melinda, the good witch, who tells her to click her heels thrice and recite the affirmation, "There's no place like home."

Fortunately for Dorothy, and to the complete satisfaction of the audience, Melinda enables the little dog to return also. Nothing environmentally has changed for Dorothy causing her to embrace her home and those around her whom she previously spurned. But it just took a trip to Oz to shake her up.

This wouldn't work for all of us. My daughter Natalie had a miserable time in Florida. Although she left Florida happy, for a lapse of time, she returned to Toronto and now she is complaining once again saying we never take her anywhere good. She'd like something more exotic and adventurous. This supposedly would make her happy.

Perhaps she is right. I believe she needs a major jolt, something like a trip to Oz. Give her a few days having nobody to talk to except scarecrows, tin men, and lions. Make her have to strive to consult some humbug wizard for directions as to how to get home. Have her pursued by a scrawny wicked witch whose shrill cackling raises her hair. I think that near the end she'd be speaking to the wizard about letting her ride home in his hot air balloon. And she wouldn't bug him about a window seat.

The question is how do I pull it off? I'm going to watch the movie carefully again for clues. If necessary, I'll consider traveling to the boonies of Kansas and changing my name to Uncle Henry. The kid has to learn.

IT'S BACK

Sometimes we lose something, then get it back eventually. But it may feel awkward to openly celebrate this victory and accordingly our rejoicing remains muted.

For example, a while back my home telephone lines went on the fritz and we had no service for about three days. Suddenly my whole life felt topsy-turvy. I just could not live without a telephone. I could only bother our neighbors to use their phones from time to time, and generally I felt totally helpless.

Most of my focus for those three days was now on my defunct phone. I felt if only my phone would work, the rest of my life would readily fall into place no problem. Hassles at work in my litigation law practice, complaints by the kids, and the economy all were dwarfed by the problem of my phoneless house.

You just don't know what it's like until it happens.

On the third day the phone guy came. The sight of his vehicle coasting down my street to me looked like the cavalry arriving just in the nick of time to rescue the fort. I almost imagined seeing Rin Tin Tin running about twenty feet in front of his van.

The service rep fixed the problem in about a half hour and to my amazement the telephone actually rang again. I asked the rep whether I could make a call and he said, "Certainly, sir."

I called my secretary at the office and my first words were, "Hello? Hello?" When I heard her voice I knew exactly how Alexander Graham Bell felt.

On top of everything, because of the nature of the problem, there was no charge for the repair.

I felt ecstatic and exhilarated. I was sailing on top of the world. En route downtown I allowed all sorts of other motorists to push in front of me. I didn't have an unkind word for any red traffic signal. Once at the office, although still in a state of happiness, I had second thoughts about trying to explain to anybody the reasons for my joy. What could I have told the receptionist when she asked why I was so cheerful?

"Hey, I feel great. My telephone works."

I just spent the rest of the day telling everyone I had won four million dollars in Lotto 649. For the time being at least my fancy was tickled to the same extent as if I had won the lotto.

So I guess I wasn't totally lying.

As you may have expected, the repair of my house telephone, although a major moral booster on the day in question, did not seem to be enough of an event to turn my life around radically and to leave me permanently in Lotus land.

In fact, one maybe even two files at work upset me albeit slightly toward the end of the day. When I drove home that evening, I still let a number of cars cut in front of me, but I was a bit more selective than I had been in the morning. Earlier I practically shouted out of my car with a blow horn asking anyone near me to get ahead if they wished. Now I had no desire to be as vocal.

And I also managed to talk to one or two red lights which had the audacity to retard my trip home, admonishing them not to do it again. Okay, maybe it was ten red lights.

The first time the phone rang that night, I grunted happily telling it not to break again. When it rang for the eighteenth time for one of my kids, I had some choice words for Alexander Graham Bell for creating this Frankenstein.

Life doesn't stand still, does it?

AS LONG AS YOU'RE HEALTHY?

If losing a telephone for a while and then regaining it brings such a surge of happiness, the situation is all the more intensive when it comes to matters of health—the ultimate subject matter for all of us.

Several years ago for several days I was discharging some funny stuff from my bronchial tubes. My first reaction was to think of the late Queen Victoria: I wasn't amused.

My family doctor referred me to a couple of specialists, and although they didn't think it was serious, they scheduled a procedure known as a bronchoscopy under a general anesthetic. As the term suggests it involves doing something similar to what Galileo did several hundred years ago, when he looked through this giant telescope and told everyone the earth was not the center of the universe.

At least this is how I understood the doctor's explanation.

I was initially terrified about the general anesthetic. I had concerns about the anesthesiologist doing what was necessary to make sure I take a return trip from wherever he was sending me. I also feared the outcome of the doctor's explorations. Look what happened after Galileo had a good look through his scope. The church excommunicated him.

A couple of days before the procedure the doctor ordered another chest X-ray. Lo and behold the radiologist saw some funny-looking shadows. I was even less amused now. The only shadows that ever amused me before were the hand shadows created by those guys who used to do wonders on the *Ed Sullivan Show,* creating the likeness of various animals and people. The most popular was General Charles de Gaulle.

The doctors weren't sure what these shadows meant. One thing for sure, the shadows bore not even a remote resemblance to le General.

The radiologist then ordered a repeat performance of the X-rays scheduled for the morning of the bronchoscopy, a day or two later. If the shadows were still there, he would do a tomogram (no relation to cookie grams). These were close-up shots.

For the next two days I felt condemned. I even drew up my will. I guess this is something I should have done in any event, especially since I had been practicing law for about five years. I never realized how close a lawyer was to home.

I couldn't eat or sleep too well. Nothing at the office seemed to matter too much. I felt about as relaxed as Ann Bolyn in the Tower of London. I did a superb job of insulating myself from the daily stresses of a law practice. I was now about the same age as Mozart was when he wrote his final symphony and this parallel also ran through my head.

The big day arrived and the doctor took the chest X-ray a couple of hours before I was to undergo the bronchoscopy. During the five minutes or so it took the radiologist to take and read the film, I was saying to myself if pulled I through this one okay, I would never worry about anything else. I meant it.

The radiologist came over, holding the film in his hand and squinting at it. He said, "It's normal. There are no shadows this time."

He couldn't explain why there had been shadows a couple of days earlier. But I was content with his ignorance. I just didn't need those shadows. I had no intentions of sending my X-rays to Ed Sullivan.

At that moment an amazing surge of happiness hit me. Here I was about to go through a bronchoscopy under a general anesthetic in an hour or two, a procedure that had been terrifying me for weeks since the day it was scheduled. Yet the coming and passing of this most recent shadow business dwarfed the terror of the next treat so much that I was now giddy and bubbly with good cheer.

I was joking around with everyone except the anesthesiologist. I didn't want to get on his bad side. This would be like Captain Kirk annoying Scotty before he beams him back.

As you've probably guessed by now, I came out of this adventure with flying colors. As you also may have guessed, I didn't keep my promise about not letting anything ever again bug me. But I sure felt super that day!

THE BANANA PEEL SYNDROME

Has anyone ever actually seen someone slip on a banana peel? I never have. In reality there are just not too many banana peels lying around on the ground for unfortunate victims to overlook and to slip on. Therefore, the question, "Why do people laugh when someone slips on a banana peel?" is moot. But the thought of it amuses people—barring injury to the victim, of course. The thought of anything going wrong for another person amuses people, even makes them happy. It shouldn't, but it does.

Natalie left Florida happy because younger brother Gabriel threw a tantrum as a result of flying back to Toronto without a window seat.

The late Yiddish comedian Shimon Dsjigan (pronounced GEE-gun) had this advice to offer his listeners. If you want to make your friends happy, put yourself into the hospital with some illness. Show them you're down and out. If, however, you're down and out on your luck and you want to depress your friends, throw a lavish party. Bring on a great show of opulence. This will upset them royally.

Notwithstanding the Ninth Commandment, the tendency of human nature is still to covet one's neighbor's wife, husband, manservant, maidservant, donkey, ass and Cadillac. Conversely, the tendency is to feel better if one hears the neighbor has had a setback or two.

During the early part of 1980 when the price of gold and silver mysteriously skyrocketed to eight hundred dollars and fifty dollars per ounce, respectively, I joined the line of thousands to help myself to the riches, buying some of each. I made the mistake of announcing this can't lose investment to a couple of friends who didn't have or want to borrow the money to also buy any and they said, "Good luck. But I wouldn't buy it. You can't get something for nothing."

When the market crashed almost overnight, silver going to about fifteen dollars per ounce, one of my friends offered his condolences. He told me he really felt sorry and he asked me not to pay any attention to his uncontrollable fit of laughter. He said he wasn't really laughing at me. Well, he certainly wasn't laughing with me because I wasn't laughing.

Comedian Bill Cosby once had a routine to the effect that while oodles of people were lining up to buy gold and silver, he hesitated and ended up not investing. He went on to say, "Then the market crashed, and I was happy."

He said it all.

THEORY OF RELATIVITY

It's not $E = MC^2$.

There are people we don't expect to be happy and yet they are. Helen Keller declared, "I have found life so beautiful."

And poet John Milton said, "The mind in its own place, and in itself, can make a heaven of hell, a hell of heaven."

Napoleon, on the other hand, claimed, "I have never known six happy days in my life."

This is incredible indeed. Napoleon was it. He had everything. And he was miserable. Helen Keller couldn't see or hear. And she was happy. And no one ever even named a pastry in her honor.

The same thing with John Milton. Whoever heard of going to a bakery and ordering a Milton? And they probably would not have allowed Milton into Maxim's either had he worn shorts. But all this didn't cheer up Napoleon. He just didn't know how good he had it.

My son Danny's minor hockey league team won the local championship when he was about twelve.

The members of the team were ecstatic as the clock ran out and the siren sounded. Their prize was a gilded-colored, plastic, foot-long hockey player. The thing looked like an Oscar. It wasn't much but the kids could not have been happier had they received the Stanley Cup or an Oscar, or both. This was happiness, the real thing, winning a championship in a peewee league in a suburb of a city that had a zillion such teams.

But now turn to Oscar night when the best actress or actor announcement is about to be made. The camera pans on five candidates. One will emerge victorious, the other four will tie for second. The camera catches all five simultaneously hoping to capture their composure when the announcement is made and the actors know this. It is at this moment when they must do their best performance, live in front of millions of people. They must create and freeze a smile on their faces and get their hands to applaud, appearing to say, "Congratulations, good show."

And maybe they should mean it, especially if they for a moment focus on the fact they are considered by the industry to be among the top five in the world.

They applaud and they may even smile but we know what they feel like inside. They feel like that poor bugger when he heard those fateful words, "Ronnie Shapiro, forty-three."

CHAPTER THREE

MONEY, MONEY, MONEY

Money makes the world go around. Or is it love that makes the world go around? I don't know what Galileo would have said about what makes the world go around. He supported Copernicus' views. Copernicus on the other hand being a monk had no use for either.

When I was a boy of about six or seven, I remember one day standing in front of the well-stocked candy counter at Mr. Cohen's Candy Store near my house. There was a kid there about my age with his father pointing at the delicacies one by one. Mr. Cohen was gleefully putting the different selections into a bag to the delight of the child.

When the kid's trip to Valhalla was over the father handed Mr. Cohen a number of coins, in an amount substantially surpassing the nickel I was clutching in my hand. The nickel was my daily allowance. As far as I was concerned I had just witnessed Donald Trump buying the moon.

When these people left the store, Mr. Cohen said to me, "And what do you want today with your nickel?" For some reason I didn't feel I had too much clout.

I thought to myself Cohen must be the luckiest guy on earth. He could help himself to the gumballs, the nuts, the licorice, or whatever his little heart desired at any time.

When I relayed my experience at the store to my dad he suggested that one day when I work and make money, I too could descend on Cohen's candy counter to my heart's delight. I decided not to wait too long.

WORK MAKES LIFE SWEET

Shortly thereafter, Montreal was hit by a blizzard that blanketed the city with several inches of snow. Many of the flats in the older sections of Montreal are triplexes, having external access by way of wrought iron staircases leading to the second and third floors, thus permitting the flats to be larger inside. But the staircases were generally impassable after a snowfall.

This is where my entrepreneurial skills came in. I decided to knock on doors offering to shovel the one or two dozen steps for a dime.

Within an hour or two I had amassed a small fortune of about fifty cents. I had visions of going to Mr. Cohen's store and getting the royal treatment, similar to how Queen Elizabeth would be treated if she were ever to walk into a dimestore. I saw myself holding a fistful of coins in front of Mr. C and he would say to the other kids, "Everyone leave the store. These candies belong to Marcel."

I hit another flat on Saint Urbain Street. I rang the doorbell and heard a woman's voice answering from behind the locked door. After I stated my business offering to clear the snow, I heard her say "yes" a couple of times. I was on a roll.

Fifteen minutes later after performing another superb job, I rang the doorbell expecting to get paid. There was no answer. I rang the bell a number of times and even banged on the door with my shovel. No luck.

I was furious standing there in the freezing weather doing my impersonation of an icicle. After a while it dawned on me I was about to experience my first bad debt. But I wasn't going to go down without a fight. If I wasn't going to get paid, the lady wasn't going to walk down the steps the way I had left them. I spent the next half hour putting back all the snow— probably more snow; all I could muster. The city road crews assigned to clean Saint Urbain Street must have wondered what strange force preceded them.

I felt good after my job had been completed. Even better than after I had removed the snow the first time. There was no change really, the snow was there, I removed it, I put it back, a bit more maybe, and I felt good. I didn't even feel the cold anymore.

At that point I thought I had put in a good day's work and I decided to pack it in. I went home and thawed out. I didn't want to tell my mother about the incident as I knew she would have gone to the lady's house with a bazooka to enforce the debt.

I thought about the incident over the years, wondering why the woman wouldn't pay me. Why she wouldn't even answer the doorbell, after saying "Yes" to me a couple of times after I asked if she wanted the snow cleared. Eventually, I found it in my heart to forgive her. Maybe she never even heard me the first time when I spoke to her. Maybe she was in bed with a companion. Perhaps the "yeses" weren't even addressed to me.

FREE MONEY

Not too long after getting introduced to the concept of bad debts, I was introduced to another lesson in high finance. The nearby bank, for a one-dollar deposit put up by my dad, gave me the use of a handsome savings cash box about the size of an electric pencil sharpener.

My father encouraged me to put whatever coins I could get my hands on into the box saying this is the way to accumulate wealth. He gave me a pitch similar to the one given in the movie *Mary Poppins* by George Banks to his son Michael when the discussion came up as to how the boy might best use his tuppence.

As Banks told Michael, if these tuppence are properly and prudently invested, they soon turn into a pound and before long this modest investment would play a role in Britain's building of foreign railroads and ocean liners.

The catch was that only the bank had the key to the box, and furthermore, the bank required my father's attendance there before its employees would open it. They told me this each time I would subsequently try to get one of them to use that magic key.

When the kitty was more or less full my father took me to the bank where the grand opening ceremony was performed. But there was another catch. I wasn't given the money. My father and the bank clerk decided the three or four dollars painstakingly saved by me should now be put into a bank account.

They tried to explain to me the concept of interest. The bank employee told me that I would give him three dollars today, and in a year he would give me back three dollars and twenty-five cents. I would get twenty five cents for "free."

Like little Michael Banks, I threw a tantrum. I didn't give a damn about railroads. I just wanted to go to Mr. Cohen's Candy Store. But my pleas went unheeded and the money went into a bank account. Unlike the result in the movie, my protests demanding my money did not cause a run on the bank by the customers of the Montreal City and District Savings Bank.

When I saw *Mary Poppins* a dozen or so years later I was so moved by that bank sequence that I loudly cheered Michael on, shouting, "Take the money and run!"

At this time I no longer remember whatever became of my money. I imagine my mind has been trying to blot out the painful memories of me getting deprived of the use thereof. I do know however that the Montreal City and District Savings Bank is no longer around. And I'm happy.

"I HADS ENOUGH AND ENOUGH IS TOO MUCH"

Popeye said that.

How much is enough money? Is there a limit one reaches at which point he or she should stop trying to accumulate more and just sit in a park under a tree and read a book?

I read a newspaper story about Bill Gates recently. Bill Gates is the thirty-something chairman of

Microsoft Corporation. According to the article he is worth fifteen billion U.S. dollars (or about 20 billion Canadian dollars). And yes, the man is still working, presumably trying to parlay this money into a fortune. What would happen if he were to put it all into the bank and live off the interest?

You will recall I am an expert in the concept of interest, having learned about it traumatically as a seven year old.

I have had to work some of this out longhand as my calculator only displays eight digits, but according to my calculations at an interest rate of 10 percent per annum, Gates would net annually 1.5 billion dollars. Paying him only for working hours, namely forty hours per week, this works out to about two thousand working hours for fifty weeks. I am giving him a two-week vacation. I hope he appreciates it. This is when he need not even think about the money his bank manager is shoveling into his account.

This works out to a neat $750,000 U.S. dollars per hour. I guess that's over one million per hour Canadian at a conversion rate of 35 percent.

I can now continue on my calculator. Dividing by thirty-six hundred, the gentleman earns $208.33 per second American. In Canada, however, that's $281.25 dollars per second. He could really do something in my country with this kind of income. Even after taxes.

What does this mean in terms of his cost of living? If he calls a plumber to unclog his blocked sink, and the plumber charges, say, fifty dollars an hour, the moment the plumber says, "Is this the place with the blocked sink?" and Gates says, "Yes," he's already earned more than the plumber's fee.

And do you think someone like Bill Gates can possibly get excited if an outfit like Domino's Pizza arrives late, thereby entitling him to a three-dollar discount? Who knows?

Although I did not agree with what George Banks did to his son Michael in *Mary Poppins* and with what my dad similarly did with my hard-earned money, I think young Bill Gates' dad ought to intervene and get Bill to put his coins into the bank to earn some of that interest.

Then again there is one thing Mr. Gates can't buy. And this is Isaac Peterson's bail tab. According to a newspaper article, it seems Mr. Peterson had been arrested seven times within a space of a couple of months in Birmingham, Alabama for burglary-related charges. The city's mayor had been criticizing District Court Judge Montgomery for setting bail too low in his court, thereby allowing habitual lawbreakers out too easily.

As one word to the wise is apparently sufficient, His Honor set bail for Isaac at 9 trillion dollars. Who cares what it works out to in Canadian. There's nobody in Canada rich enough to pay this guy's bail. And not only can't I put this number on my calculator, I don't even know what it looks like on paper. I feel like Ronnie Shapiro.

By the way, in case you're interested, Isaac is still trying to make bail.

MORE NUMBERS

I have no use for statistics. Any expert can divide almost anything into anything else and write a paper about it.

Noted humorist Stephen Leacock wrote a piece once about the average Canadian. There was a comment in the article to the effect that judges have handed out jail sentences to Canadians totaling about ten thousand years. He then divided this figure by the population in Canada and he concluded that the average Canadian has spent about two weeks of his life in jail.

And what use do we have for the common demographic and sociological stats telling us each couple has 1.8 children?

Barry, a lawyer friend of mine, takes statistics seriously. He figures he bills his clients 225 dollars per hour. (If it seems outrageous, remember what Bill Gates makes while on automatic pilot.) I once asked Barry to spend a few extra minutes with me at lunch suggesting he have a second cup of tea. He looked at his watch and told me that second cup would take ten minutes to drink and therefore it would cost him twenty-two dollars and fifty cents. He simply couldn't afford it.

I then tried to make the situation more palatable for him. I asked, "Barry, your partner gets fifty percent?"

"Yeah, that's true," he agreed.

"So the tea will only cost you eleven-twenty-five," I calculated.

He nodded his approval. I then added, "Of the money you earn, you pay about fifty percent for taxes?"

"Uh hmm," he affirmed, after taking a couple of puffs on his pipe.

"So it's really only costing you two-sixty-three for that second cup?"

My Socratic reasoning was winning out, I felt.

Then Barry continued. "But it would still cost me seventy cents for the tea."

I agreed. Added to the two-sixty-three this was a total of three-thirty-three for that second cup.

I couldn't dispute the fact.

He continued, "And in order for me to earn three-thirty-three net after taxes, I've got to bill six dollars and sixty-six cents."

I couldn't have agreed more.

We both noticed a student sitting next to us having a tea and it was costing him only seventy cents. Barry and I agreed, however, he would have to pay almost seven bucks or ten times this amount for that cup of tea. I quickly took a sip of my tea, and we stormed out of the restaurant. We both now clearly understood and appreciated the motivation of those American colonists who over two hundred years ago instigated the Boston tea party.

FEWER NUMBERS . . . ALL THAT GLITTERED STOPPED GLITTERING

It was the end of 1979 and the beginning of 1980. There were no fancy statistics this time. The price of gold and silver were going in only one direction, up. Gold started its rise in the three hundred range and was soon to hit eight hundred dollars an ounce. Silver had started below ten dollars and was soon to reach fifty U.S. dollars.

I was never one to care about investments. I always shunned anything financial. To me the name Wall Street has the same ring and allure as Alcatraz. I was always more interested in Sesame Street.

That fateful day in January as silver was into the forties per ounce, I decided to take action. Rumors were blazing that before long it would be hitting a C note per ounce. I calculated I could therefore better than double my money easily by buying silver now. I had been in touch with the silver fix by calling this bank number where a tape would give you the hourly rate. That day alone it had gone up about a buck an hour. The last time I called the voice on the tape had merely said, "Don't bug me. I'm out buying silver."

It was three-thirty in the afternoon and I decided to get in now. I snuck out of the office giving some inconspicuous excuse like my wife was having a baby.

I ran to my bank and cleaned out forty-five hundred dollars in cash. I then jogged over to the trust company selling precious metals and not surprisingly there was a long line of people inside, with some overflow potential investors lined up outside. A security guard was letting outside people through the door as customers who had already dropped their savings for the metals were leaving. The place was closing at four.

There were a couple of dozen of us standing outside, freezing in the January cold. One guy said, "Not to worry. With the killing we make, we'll all be able to take a trip to the Caribbean."

Everyone agreed. Sounded good to me. I just prayed I would get into the place before it closed.

We were all quite jealous of those lucky people who had already been let into the bank by the security guard. One potential customer said, "It's no fair. They can't just serve the guys already inside. Our money is just as good."

I let out an "ugh" in unison with the other freezing stiffs in agreement with this comment.

The guard let me in just before four. I felt like I had just won a lottery. I didn't realize that in fact I was about to follow the Pied Piper.

Once inside, company staff announced they would stay open a bit longer but only to service those already inside. By then about a hundred people were still in line outside, no doubt planning their trips south. About two minutes later the place closed its doors to the public, several minutes ahead of schedule in view of the large crowd. When the mob outside saw the doors clang shut they all shouted, "Foul." Some people were banging on the doors.

The security guard tried to calm them down but to no avail. He quickly backed into the bank after he realized if the crowd wasn't going to get some gold or silver, they might go for other precious substances, like his jewels.

The spectacle reminded me of a scene in Shakespeare's *Julius Caesar*. The mob of Romans had been greatly moved by the eloquent speech of Mark Anthony who had just asked them to give him their ears and who had just made them feel terribly guilty for their sympathies to the assassination of big Juli. They now recant their views and are ready to tear to shreds any of the conspirators who should stumble across their paths. Lo and behold they run across Sinna. Not Sinna the conspirator but Sinna the poet, a gentleman whose only unfortunate connection with the bad guys is his name.

That's good enough for the mob who, nevertheless, proceeds to summarily disembowel him, notwithstanding the poet's desperate attempts to explain this amusing coincidence. Let me tell you, this mob outside was more hostile.

We fortunate ones inside simply couldn't understand the apparent edginess of those people out there. They were acting like animals. Making all this fuss merely because they couldn't buy some gold or silver. My word! Get a life!

My turn came and I paid my forty-five hundred dollars. In return I received a silver certificate for a hundred ounces. All I had to do now was go home and wait for the price of silver to go to one hundred dollars per ounce, which according to the experts, was after dinner that night. I left the place to the accompaniment of sneers from some of the frozen stiffs who hadn't managed to buy today. From the look they gave me, I knew exactly how that other mother felt after King Solomon handed the mystery baby to the first mother.

The next morning I woke up expecting to be greeted by news that silver was now sixty to seventy dollars per ounce. I couldn't get through to the tape. I thought maybe the guy went back to the trust company to line up. To my surprise the fix was forty-one dollars per ounce. Although shocked initially, the reason given by the experts was "profit taking." But all was well. I was led to believe I could still buy my tickets to the Caribbean.

The next couple of days saw the metal drop into the thirties. This time the reason was given as "market adjustment."

So far, I had lost almost a thousand dollars or twenty percent of my investment in a couple of days. But this didn't bug me as much as the visions I had of the people in that mob who never got in and who now must have been splitting their guts with laughter. Meanwhile, I felt like Sinna. The poet.

The metal soon dropped into the twenties. At this point my former stockbroker and financial advisor introduced me to another brilliant concept: loss averaging.

He said, "Just buy another hundred ounces at twenty-five dollars an ounce. This way once it hits thirty-seven-fifty, you'll break even."

The principle sounded good to me as I was standing in line once again this time wearing a pair of dark sunglasses. All that had to happen was for the metal to go up to thirty-seven-fifty. And then again all the Anaheim Mighty Ducks needed to win the Stanley Cup was to first get into the playoffs.

After I bought in at twenty-five, it dropped again within days into the teens. The experts ran the profit taking and market adjustment routines on us again.

I always liked that profit taking one. I gave my former stockbroker a tongue lashing why he never told me to take profits as the market was about to plummet. I always wondered who took profits, and how they knew when to take them.

Soon there was also talk of some multimillionaire brothers from Texas called the Hunts who had somehow manipulated the silver market causing the price to skyrocket artificially. I didn't understand or care about the theories or excuses. I wasn't angry at the Hunt brothers. I only wished if indeed they were responsible for the silver crash, that after they meet

61

St. Peter one day, instead of going to that hot place they would be chained to a polar ice cap with nothing to wear but their ten-gallon hats.

I eventually sold my silver for twelve dollars an ounce. The rate today is about six. How's that for profit taking?

I am not a gambler. For better or for worse I believe there's no such thing as a free lunch, unless I guess you're in jail. Good appetite, Isaac Peterson.

PLEASE TAKE THE 10 MILLION DOLLARS

A while back I received in the mail a letter from some publishing outfit indicating I had won ten million dollars. Or at least I was a finalist, one of three, selected to qualify. The letter went on to say that if interested, all I had to do was return the envelope with a little enclosed green disk marked "yes".

If I didn't give a damn about the ten million, the letter asked me still to return the envelope with the red disk marked "no." In this case I would still receive a consolation prize, something like a Cadillac Seville.

I had just ten days to respond or I would lose it all.

I opted just to throw the whole package, which included photographs and stories about other previous winners, into the garbage. It's not that I couldn't use the ten million dollars. My youngest son Gabriel wanted me to buy him a new Lego set, so I had some motivation to respond. But I passed.

A few weeks later I received another package in the mail. The letter read in part as follows:

Dear Mr. Strigberger,

Although you did not respond one way or the other to our first offer, and even though the deadline for replying is long past, we had a board of directors meeting here at Give It Away Publishing and the board unanimously agreed to extend the deadline to the end of the month. So, Mr. Strigberger, you must act now. To make the proposition more attractive, we have even eliminated one of the other lucky contestants who were competing against you.

We look forward to receiving your "yes" disk in the mail . . .

I noticed my name was plastered all over the letter and the enclosures. It appeared several times in the letter and on the brochure among the list of instant millionaires whose pictures were printed. In fact, the photograph had four or five couples about to walk up the gangplank of some cruise ship resembling the *Love Boat* and the caption had those people saying, "Please join us, Marcel."

I passed this time too. I didn't even return the "no" disk even though my guaranteed consolation prize was sweetened to include a chauffeur to drive that Seville. In fact the Seville in the folder had a personalized license plate that read "Strig."

I was quite happy with my Chevrolet Celebrity. And I was quite competent and happy to drive it myself. I went on with life.

Not too long ago I received yet another letter from you know who. It read as follows:

Dear Mr. Strigberger,

We note we still haven't heard from you.

Charlie of our Public Relations Department thought perhaps you might think our offer to you is a gimmick. To show you it isn't a gimmick, we are pleased to advise you that we have eliminated your other competitor and we are enclosing a photocopy of your ten million dollar check. To get the original just return the "yes" disk.

Or if you don't want the money, just return the "no" disk.

Your Seville along with Sydney, the chauffeur, is waiting.

There are no magazines or books to buy, if you don't want to. Guaranteed . . .

I know these people are out to sell me magazine subscriptions. So I responded by returning the "yes" disk and ordering a hundred dollars worth of magazines, of their choice, and asking them to send me 9,999,900 dollars in change. (I don't know what that works out to per second.)

I have good news. I called the outfit last week about my 9,999,900 dollars and they told me the check was in the mail.

CHAPTER FOUR

WAR AND PEACE

This chapter has nothing to do with Tolstoy.

BORN ON A MOUNTAINTOP IN TENNESSEE

During the mid-1950s, every kid had his or her eyes glued to the television watching *Walt Disney,* or whatever the show was called. There was a three-part feature entitled "Davy Crockett." Every kid was wearing a racoon-tailed fur cap as he or she watched the final episode. And final it was.

The hero was on top of the ramparts of the Alamo swinging his musket, "Old Betsy", frantically in circular maneuvers trying to club as many Mexicans as he could rather than give up the fort.

We never saw him get killed as a dozen or so Mexican soldiers dressed like the toy soldiers in *The Nutcracker* surround Davy and are about to do a piñata on him. The kids watching knew it didn't look good for Davy Crockett, king of the wild frontier.

As we grew up we discovered that yes indeed, Davy Crockett bit the dust at the Alamo. I was one of the kids who later asked the question, "Why?"

The building was a hundred-year-old mission of no strategic importance to anyone. Texan leader Sam Houston indicated earlier the place was indefensible against a rush of five thousand Mexican troops. And yet a couple hundred yahoos decided to cash out at the Alamo. Why?

I guess for what it's worth, today they're heroes, of a sort. But the Mexicans lost about fifteen hundred men. What about these guys? Do you think there's a plaque somewhere in Mexico today commemorating the fifteen hundred suckers who lost their lives while bravely trying to wrestle some useless old ruin from one hundred and ninety screaming Texans?

I think both sides ought to have had their heads examined. If the Texans wanted to prove a point and risk their lives, notwithstanding Sam Houston's caution, then the Mexicans should simply have let them be. Let them stay at the Alamo all they want. Not attack them. See if the Texans, expecting a good fight, wouldn't get bored.

Mexican Commander Santa Anna could just have gone about his business without taking a detour at the Alamo for a couple of weeks. It would have been interesting to listen in on the bravado occupants at the Alamo:

COMMANDER TRAVIS: You boys reckon them Mexicans are comin' back?

JAMES BOWIE: Don't know, Travis. It's been two months since we last saw any of them taco eaters.

TRAVIS:	Bowie, why don't you go out there and see what's doin'. And don't forget your knife.
CROCKETT:	I'll come with you, Jim. The two of us, your knife and Old Betsy can handle Santa Anna and his men, no problem.
GEORGE RUSSELL:	Want me to come too, Davy?
CROCKETT:	Sure, Georgie. You can take care of the prisoners.

I don't know to what extent history would have been rewritten, but one thing for sure, the word Alamo to most people would have only meant a car rental outfit.

YOU'RE A . . .

> Tweedledum and Tweedledee
> agreed to have a battle.
> 'Cause Tweedledum, said
> Tweedledee had spoiled his
> brand new rattle
>
> —*Lewis Carroll*

I firmly believe there is a myth abounding as to what the oldest profession is. The truth is the oldest profession is fighting. People have to strive to beat one another in some form or another.

The world was just in its infancy in biblical times when Cain didn't like the fact that his brother Abel was making a clean sweep of it as far as pleasing the Lord with his sacrifices. Abel's offerings were all accepted instantly whereas Cain's were about as popular as the Edsel. Cain could have and should have just walked away and taken over the rest of the earth, which at this juncture was his for the taking. He could even have taken over all of Saudi Arabia and Kuwait.

Instead he decided to bludgeon his only brother. Perhaps he would not have physically abused Abel had there been some games invented at the time, like chess. In that case he might have said to his brother, "When you're finished with that ram, come here and I'll whip your ass with my newly developed Euphrates Queen Pawn Attack."

Unfortunately for Abel there were no games around in those days. Bad timing.

On second thought, however, it is possible that Abel would have been a better chess player than Cain. Abel could have said at one point, "So much for your newly developed Euphrates Queen Pawn Attack. Set the pieces up again when you're ready for me. Now let me get back to the altar and send up a few more winners."

In that case I think the result would have been the same.

THE STRUGGLE OF THE PROLETARIAT, AND EVERYONE ELSE

I think men (meaning men, women, persons, people, human beings, and all reasonable facsimiles) just have to struggle. It's natural for any place to break up into a north and a south or an east and a west and for a struggle to ensue.

Although the Soviet Union has become extinct, look at the struggle between the Russians and the

Chechnians. And then there is the dispute between Russia and the Ukraine. They have both been arguing over who should take charge of the fleet of hundreds of naval ships in the Baltic Sea.

The Ukrainian defense minister insists the Ukraine needs these ships for its defense.

Now who in his right mind is going to launch an amphibious attack on the shores of the Ukraine? Some junkie for cabbage rolls?

CHILE, EAST VERSUS WEST

I always enjoyed studying geography. I love looking at a large globe trying to imagine what places look like. The country that fascinates me the most, geographically speaking, is Chile. On the map its shape almost resembles an earthworm in a vertical position. It looks like its about three thousand miles long and twenty miles wide. My impression is probably not too far from reality.

I know very little about Chile except that it's not safe to make fun of its leaders. But I'm willing to bet there is a split between the different regions. I don't only mean north and south. I mean east and west, width wise. I'll bet the inland easterners poke fun at the pacific coastal westerners calling them "a bunch of fishermen." No doubt the westerners in turn consider themselves rugged and weatherworn, like the Vikings. Western Chile must just be inundated with jokes about how eastern Chileans are landlubbing sissies. A coastal woman has her father to contend with if she wants to run off and marry a farmer from the east. And the boy living in the east, meanwhile has to think of a way of explaining this proposed marriage to his own father, finding a way to interrupt him while he is cracking up at the joke just made by the neighbor that started out as, "How many westerners does it take to . . .?"

And you think the respective families of Romeo and Juliet had problems?

This isn't about Chile; it's about mankind (meaning mankind, womankind, etc.).

CRUSADES. VOLUNTEERS NEEDED. INFIDELS NEED NOT APPLY.

People just can't leave well enough alone. Some nine hundred years ago all of Europe decided to gang up and liberate the Holy Land from the infidel Moslems. Big shots from an assortment of countries, regions, fiefdoms, and duchies (not the donuts) got together and with the Pope's blessings they set off for the Middle East in the name of the Lord.

And what happened when the first Crusade arrived? Did Saladin, the leader of the bad guys, say to his people, "We've been here long enough folks. These men with big red crosses painted on their tunics are asking us to vacate Jerusalem. Since we are just a bunch of infidels anyway, let's just pack up and leave."

To the surprise of the good guys, the infidels resisted. And they resisted the second crusade, and the third one, too.

King Richard the Lion-Hearted, who was one of the nicer players of the campaign, almost lost his throne to his brother, big bad John, who stayed behind in England to mind the store and take from the poor and give to the rich. Heaven only knows what would have happened had Robin of Locksley, alias Robin Hood, not made it back from the crusades in time. There's no telling what John and his stooge, the Sheriff of Nottingham, would have done.

Then again it's sort of frightening to think the destiny of England was altered by a group of merry men running around the forest in leotards.

ONE GIANT STEP

The only sensible battle I could think of was the one between David and Goliath. At least in this case the parties were rational enough to each pick a champion to slug it out, winner take all. This no doubt saved the lives of battalions of soldiers who probably had no hard feelings toward one another to start with, but who otherwise would have had to spend the afternoon impaling one another.

What impresses me the most about the duel was not that little David won. Hey, after all, the man upstairs (man meaning man, woman, spirit, etc.— this is the last time I'll do this) was on his side. The big trick here was that once Goliath came crashing down with a headache, the Philistines, who vastly outnumbered the Hebrews, kept their part of the bargain and said, "Okay, we're out of here. Fair is fair. It's cricket."

The number two man could just as well have said, "Hey, wait a minute. There's nothing in writing confirming this deal." Lucky thing for the Hebrews there were no lawyers around, yet.

BUT WHY, PRAY TELL?

The next question is why do people have to struggle with one another?

I imagine the obvious answer is to achieve a material goal. I would say this is the driving force of a bank robber, although I do not think he quite runs it through his mind this way. "Why do I come to the bank with this gun? I have this material goal: money."

I also imagine that if I had the means as a young lad, I would also have hit the bank in this manner to get my savings out.

On a larger scale, certain people who should know better sometimes attack other countries to seize and possess them. History is full of the likes of the Goths, the Visigoths, the Helvetians, the Huns, the Moors, and other assorted gangs that lost no sleep in raiding more peaceful groups that were content to simply be left alone and maybe do some fishing, like the western Chileans.

For centuries the Romans were the champions in conquering. And wherever they conquered they brought their entertainment, including gladiator fights and lion-taming events. Unfortunately, the tamers weren't too experienced and had to learn hands-on. Usually, without a chair and a whip.

I have fond memories of my eighth-grade Latin class. We studied from a book originally published in 1934 entitled, *Latin for Today*. The exercise in Latin was about the map of ancient Europe. The story ran through a number of countries reading, *"Gallia est barbara, Germania est Barbara . . ."*

But Rome, on the other hand was not uncivilized, the exercise went on to say.

I don't know. My ancestors in what is Israel today were crucified, sold into slavery, and sent into arenas to try to reason with ravenous leos. I would hate see what might have happened to them had the Romans been uncivilized.

IT'S IMMATERIAL

Sometimes the goal of the aggressors is not material gain. It could be adventure or glory. The Alamo. Old Betsy and all that.

Or General Custer at Little Big Horn. This guy was even a greater strategist than the leader of the Alamo. At least they were in a fortress waiting for company. Custer just went out into the open to confront a much larger group of Sioux. My sole question is where did Custer muster his confidence? You might recall that song of the sixties about one of his men which goes, "Please, Mr. Custer, I don't want to go." How is it that so often the yo-yos in life become the leaders?

REVENGE

Then again conflict could stem from the urge for revenge. Or whatever one will call it to rationalize it.

I'll never forget the day in fifth-grade Jewish study class when Henry Waxman stupidly pulled away a chair from behind another kid, Marvin Dorfman. Although Dorfman wasn't hurt, he collected all two hundred pounds of himself and charged straight for Waxman, planning no doubt to flatten him. As the Dorfman grabbed the startled Waxman in a headlock the two of them tumbled to the floor. The rabbi quickly intervened. Lifting Marvin Dorfman off at the expense of probably getting a herniated disk, he pleaded, "Enough Marvin. Don't you know it's a sin to take revenge?"

Without skipping a beat Dorfman replied, "Rabbi, I'm not taking revenge. I just want to get even."

Isn't it all a matter of perspective? One's own perspective.

Getting back to those Latin lessons. We learned that the Romans eventually worked their way northeast where they took over England. After a respite they headed further north against the Scots. The book said they weren't out to conquer the Scots, they just went there to "subdue" them.

When I studied that lesson I had visions of fifty thousand screaming madmen running around in kilts, throwing tantrums, and breaking windows. The Roman emperor figured he'd better put an end to this nonsense and so he sent his legions up to Scotland carrying chariot loads of Valium.

Today the Scots still seem to have a bit of a feud going between the Campbells and the MacDonalds as a result of a number the Campbells did on the Macs a couple of hundred years ago.

When my wife and I visited a medieval church in Edinborough, the guide said solemnly, "If there are any Campbells in the group and you want to pay tribute to a great Campbell, then head over to the crypt by the east wall where you will find the tomb of Sir So-and-So Campbell."

The guide added, in a completely turned around and jovial tone, "If on the other hand there are any MacDonalds in this group, and you want to visit the tomb of a Campbell rogue and scoundrel . . ."

Is anybody ever wrong?

IT'S MATERIAL AND IMMATERIAL

Some wars will result as a combination of the practical and tangible and the esoteric.

The English and the French always had a thing about one another. The Norman big shots living in England in the 1300s remembered that William the First, the guy who started it all, arrived from France in 1066 and conquered England after winning the Battle of Hastings. After three hundred years or so there was very little French about William's ancestors other than the French calling a leg of lamb *mouton* and the English calling it mutton.

This was enough to convince the English there was still this great bond between themselves and their roots in France. They decided to cross the channel and help themselves to *La Belle France.*

They did quite well for many years, winning battle after battle. While the French archer tried to load his crossbow, a feat that required the strength of Arnold Schwarzenegger, the English bowman would fire off ten deadly arrows with his longbow.

Things didn't look too good for the French until about a hundred years from the time of the first shot, when Joan of Arc, the handmaiden of Orléans, heard some voices and told the French it was going to be all right. She rallied the French forces and helped liberate France. Don't ask me where all those great English bowmen were then.

But I don't like the fact that the English apprehended Joan and burned her at the stake as a witch. The English had this thing about witch burning, still carrying over this tradition centuries later into Salem, Massachusetts. Considering that the British drive on the left-hand side of the road, they have an inexplicable intolerance for eccentrics.

To this day I am annoyed at the roasting of Ms. Arc. Surely they could have just kept her for a future prisoner trade deal? Something like, "We'll give you back the witch if you return Philip the Fat." It's just a suggestion.

Fortunately, the war ended quickly after a mere hundred years. I get the feeling, however, the French and the English still didn't care for one another. No matter what, there is one thing the English could never have—good weather. And this may have been one of the chief forces motivating the English to conquer other lands—to enjoy some sun.

The Hundred Years' War ended, leaving tens of thousands of soldiers dead and nobody happy. Both sides left the war thinking, as Yogi Bear would say, "I'll get you in the next cartoon."

LA BELLE PROVINCE

The next cartoon was four hundred years later in Quebec.

It's not that the French had this inalienable right to the place to start with. Let us remember who lived in New France for centuries before Jacques Cartier arrived in Montreal in 1535, planted a cross, and claimed everything everywhere for the king of France.

Today while the Québécois leaders are talking separation from Canada, native leaders are busy giving the French-Canadians remedial lessons in history. They claim they don't remember sending an invite to

Mr. Cartier asking him to come to the shores of the St. Lawrence and help civilize the place.

Nor was Chief Donnacona terribly amused after nursing Cartier and his men back to health during a terribly cold winter, that old Jacques showed his appreciation by kidnaping one of the chief's sons to France in order to convince the king that yes, there is life west of Bordeaux.

The British, however, felt their presence in the area was needed to set things right.   Two hundred years later the British weren't doing too badly having acquired the thirteen colonies to the south, including Boston. (I mention Boston because it is one of my favorite cities. I'll tell you more about this later when I discuss why people need one another after all.) At this time some ambitious souls in England figured they were on a roll. They had just finished decimating the Scottish clans up north at the Battle of Culloden, brilliantly outgunning the Scottish swordsmen. How's that for cricket!

It was also a feat the Romans could never achieve, being too fearful of the fierce Scots some seventeen hundred years earlier. The Roman commander and his legions ventured north of Chester, took a few cohorts across the border, got their hides tanned, and sent a messenger back to Rome saying, "These guys are wild. They turned our boys into McNuggets. I say we just stay in England and enjoy the weather."

The king of England noticed all those Canadian beaver pelts finding their way to the royal courts of Europe. And he no doubt remembered the drubbing his ancestors' forces received at the hands of Joan of Arc and company. He figured the time was ripe: *We'll get those frogs once and for all.*

77

And so General James Wolfe was appointed to do the job and capture Quebec. He actually came close to not succeeding as he couldn't figure out a way to get his men and guns up the cliffs of Quebec City. His big fear was waiting too long and winter coming along thereby trapping his fleet in the icy St. Lawrence. Wouldn't that have left the general with egg on his face?

I've never seen it happen, but I imagine the French forces would have walked down the hill onto the icy river. Then they would have approached the British ships one by one and knocked, saying, "Excuse me, is this boat taken?" Think of shooting fish in a barrel.

The best the British could have done at this stage would have been to invite the French aboard for some hot tea. The Quebec tea party. History would not have been the same.

As it happened, there was this perennial traitor who told the English of this secret path which was never guarded and which could be scaled by Wolfe, his men, their cannon, and their horses in about three minutes. The French would be baffled by this surprise advance and the battle would be over in minutes.

It always amazes me how history repeats itself and how so many people don't appreciate and learn from this phenomena.

Wasn't there also a traitor among the Spartans two thousand years earlier? As I recall while the three hundred Spartans were cleaning the floor up with the ten zillion Persians at the passes of Thermopylae, holding them off for days just fine, some slouch squealed to the Persians about this secret path. At least that's the way it happened in the movie I saw as a kid, entitled *The Three Hundred Spartans.* (What else?)

You would have expected the French to learn from history and rationalize better. French General Louis Joseph Montcalm defending Quebec should have gotten off his white horse and said, "There is no way these English puddings can get up here by a frontal attack. From here we can hold them off forever."

(Wolfe apparently tried to bombard the fortified city from the middle of the river by lobbing cannon balls from his ships. This wasn't going to help get his men up and capture the city but the general had to make his presence known with a show of force. The cannonballs landing in the water short of the shores really got the French scared.)

As Montcalm was saying, "We can hold out just like those Spartans. Hey, wait a minute. That secret path. What if there is a traitor among us? Nah. On the other hand, Leonides the Spartan didn't guard that path either at Thermopylae. I better not take a chance. Who knows, maybe Wolfe promised one of my men a handsome reward for revealing some topographical secrets. Maybe a couple of British damsels, or an autographed copy of *Hamlet.* I'd better fortify and guard that secret path right now."

And this, my friends, would have done it. No British in Canada, no talk today of Quebec separation. I guess General Montcalm never saw that Spartan movie.

BIRDS DO IT . . . BEES DO IT

I was in Switzerland once staring at the Alps (what else?). What do I see shooting through the skies? A squadron of Mirage jet fighters.

I was curious what these suckers running at a few million dollars a crack were doing flying over Switzerland. I thought initially perhaps the Swiss were using them for aerobatics, to entertain all the tourists standing in line waiting to catch a cable car up another mountain.

After all why would a neutral country need an air force? The last time anybody ever took a shot at a Swissman was seven hundred years ago when William Tell aimed his crossbow and made apple sauce out of the apple on his son's head.

I believe the Swiss leader at that point said, "Weapons are dangerous. Switzerland is becoming neutral. Let the French and the English fight. War is cuckoo. Hey, let's call these new clocks . . ."

Further inquiry lead me to discover that indeed, although neutral, Switzerland had several hundred warplanes in its arsenal. All males are eligible to be drafted into the forces where they serve a term of a year or two.

I didn't find out much more at the time. Years later a client of mine who immigrated to Canada from Switzerland confirmed to me that he himself had spent his shift in the forces. When I pried further, he looked around the room and lowering his voice to a whisper told me that while in the army they taught him to sneak behind enemy lines, do lots of damage, and return.

Imagine, I had in front of me a real live former Swiss commando. Manfred wouldn't tell me more, no matter how persistent I was. The more I insisted it was really okay he disclose all the Swiss tactics and military objectives to me, the more he tried to change the subject. He wouldn't even tell me who these enemies might be. Or what damage he would do.

All I could envisage is a band of men dressed in lederhosen and feathered caps and closely resembling Kurt and Friederich Von Trapp. I imagined them sneaking into neighboring France, descending on the city of Dijon, and breaking a barrel of mustard.

I even asked Manfred, "Fred, is that it? The mustard?"

His lips were sealed. I couldn't even get him to tell me more when I suggested as his lawyer representing him in his car accident case I must know everything about his previous physical endeavors. All he gave me was his name and serial number. He told me he relied on the Geneva Convention. Specifically, Section 56B(iv) which regulates how much information about your commando activities you have to give your own lawyer.

I still am amazed about the Swiss. How do you become neutral? Isn't neutrality great? Nobody, not even Hitler, ever attacks you. What if everyone would declare neutrality? Would nobody attack anybody else? It's a thought.

MY CONFESSION

Closer to home I am proud to say I have always been a peace-loving person. I have always bent over backward to avoid a fight. I never assaulted anyone for no reason at all except once, right after the 1956 Hungarian revolution.

The attempted revolt against the Russians failed miserably resulting in thousands of Hungarians fleeing Hungary and setting up shop and home throughout the world. One of these people was Tibor, whose family had moved to Montreal. Generally speaking, I had no problems with that.

But Tibor wore this funny-looking hat. It had a leather top with a ear flaps snapped on which he could then unsnap and lower and fasten by tieing the string under his chin. Seeing that he barely spoke English, I declared his hat a blatant act of provocation. I would have warned him to remove his hat but I didn't speak a word of Hungarian. Nor was I going to learn any. As Tibor was also my neighbor, I couldn't really avoid seeing the offending hat daily as he stood on his porch and watched me play street hockey with my friends. In fact on one occasion I was playing goal and I let in about ten shots. Each time some of the kids would laugh and cheer, so would Tibor, still wearing that hat.

I knew the sole reason I had let in those goals was that Tibor had deliberately spooked me. His hat. I had had enough. There is only so much a man could take. The time for diplomacy was over. I would have to take firm action lest my hockey career go down the tubes.

After I let in my twelfth goal for the afternoon, I looked at Tibor expecting him to be rolling on his porch. To my surprise he wasn't laughing. He just shrugged his shoulders. But I was sure he was splitting at the seams on the inside. He was doing an excellent con job on me trying to show regret. I went over to him to teach him a lesson. And I was going to do something once and for all about his provocative hat. I was going to confiscate it. I guess I wasn't employing the element of surprise in my favor. I didn't think I needed it.

As Tibor saw me approaching, he stood and smiled. The gall of this kid I thought. I grabbed his hat and flipped it like a Frisbee into the snow. Now that you know me better I must confess I have done this diabolical act once.

Tibor's smile vanished. He then grabbed me by the lapels and slapped me across the cheeks twice, the way Scarlett O'Hara hit Rhett Butler when he told her he knew she loved Ashley most.

In the limited bit of English Tibor knew, he said, "Why you throw my hat off?"

I looked at him and I searched my brain for an answer. I retorted with a brilliant bit of repartee, "I don't know, Tibor." I felt weird, as if a lightning bolt had struck me. I apologized, after retrieving his hat and cleaning off the snow.

I don't know what had possessed me all along to have contempt for the kid and what made me snap out of it. To this day I have never relived the senseless contempt that I had felt all along for Tibor. I have never felt the urge to assail someone because I didn't like what they looked or what they sounded like.

Tibor and I subsequently became good friends. We spent several years playing hockey together, each of us aspiring to play in the NHL. As a teen his family moved to California and I never saw him again. I guess he never made it to the big league either. I don't remember his family name but I don't know of any NHL player ever called "Tibor."

Upon reflection I am delighted this experience happened. It taught me a lesson. And I certainly hope the angel Gabriel will cut me some slack around judgment time. I can just see him hitting that keyboard and up comes, "Sins . . . Strigberger, Marcel . . . Montreal 1957 . . . flipped Tibor's hat . . ."

I trust the good angel will hit "Delete."

PEACE

The great war

That's what they called World War I.

We remember the horrors of the great one every November 11 at 11 A.M. That's when all the shooting stopped.

But did you know the final peace deal was concluded in a railway car in France around five in the morning? The powers that were, however, for some inexplicable reason decided the peace would take effect at 11 A.M. and that for the next six hours it would be business as usual.

It also seems that as a result of this fervor for peace another couple of thousand soldiers got killed or wounded that morning. Why couldn't they just have shook hands in the caboose and spread the word to lay down their arms?

I imagine that had the soldiers in the trenches on both sides known about the recently concluded deal, they would have considered stall tactics for the next few hours. If I had been there I know I would have turned to my commanding officer and said, "I can't fight anymore. I've just developed flat feet."

If that would not have worked, I would have embraced him and kissed him on the lips. Hey, peace was around the corner. Wasn't it time for love?

Good news is not news

Ongoing peace generally does not make much news. Of course the end of a war makes banner headlines. But the existence of peace is taken for granted.

For example, Canada and the United States have beaten their swords into plowshares vis-à-vis one another since the conclusion of the 1812–1814 war. We have the longest unguarded border in the world. Is there anyone who doesn't take this phenomena for granted?

Why doesn't CNN spend a couple of minutes a day out of its twenty-four-hour broadcast focusing on this peace? I'd like to see them utilize Wolf Blitzer, who during the Gulf War against Iraq seemed to be awake for forty days and forty nights interviewing and reporting the details of the war, now report on the peace:

Good morning ladies and gentlemen, this is Wolf Blitzer reporting from Queenston Ontario, ten miles from Niagara Falls on the frontier between Canada and the United States. This town saw a vigorous battle in 1814 in which British General Isaac Brock fell after a valiant fight. A two-hundred-foot cylindrical monument on the fields of Queenston Heights commemorates the battle between two former enemies who are now friends and who have never engaged in war since. I have spoken to a few people near the border today to inquire where this peace is going. With us now is Charlie Wiggly who owns a fudge shop nearby. Mr. Wiggly, what do you think about the peace?

WIGGLY: Well Wolf, it is certainly still holding.

CNN: What do you expect the next move of the Americans to be?

WIGGLY: That's hard to say Wolf. We're keepin' our eyes and ears open. But we don't expect them to attack again.

CNN: Are you taking any steps as a results of the peace?

WIGGLY: Funny you should ask. We actually plan to open a second fudge store in nearby Niagara-on-the-Lake, next to old Fort George. We thought ten years ago maybe we should give peace a couple more years to see whether it was holding. Why don't you come over in a couple of months for some free fudge?

CNN: Thank you Charlie.

WIGGLY: Thank you, Wolf.

Frankly, I don't see this happening. There's a greater likelihood of the Maytag repairman getting a service call. But I like the thought.

CHAPTER FIVE

MD, PHD AND OTHER D'S

DAMN IT JIM, I'M A DOCTOR

Even centuries into the future aboard the starship *Enterprise,* the doctor occupies a spot at the top of the ladder. Dr. McCoy ("Bones") doesn't carry around the traditional black bag but we all know that with his training he can do a heart transplant, by simply looking at the patient, in about two minutes while Captain Kirk and company are busy warding off a battalion of vicious Klingons.

For my third birthday present I received a tonsillectomy. On my dining room table. In Antwerp, Belgium, where I was born.

I had been expecting a birthday party that day. Instead, after being starved inexplicably during the morning, at about high noon in walked Dr. Van Baaten, the caricature of a doctor. He was in his fifties, blackish-gray hair, spectacles, a three-piece gray suit, a black bag, and a lack of emotion. I had remembered occasional exposure to him in the past and to me he may as well have been Nazi fiend Joseph Mengele. What else would a kid call an old man who squeezes you without asking if it's okay, who forces sticks into your mouth, and who pokes painful needles into your arm? Mother Theresa?

The operation went as planned after Joseph and his nurse readily subdued my valiant efforts to resist the administration of the anesthetic, the alcohol smell of which I recall to this day.

When I moved to Montreal a year later, Dr. Van Baaten was replaced by Dr. Bloom. He was a gentleman in his fifties, a black bag, blackish-gray hair, spectacles . . . you know the rest.

Dr. Bloom was almost a clone of Dr. Van B. In retrospect it all reminded me of the movie *The Boys of Brazil* in which an evil genius physician played by Gregory Peck cloned a number of little boys using some of Hitler's best qualities.

I wasn't in Canada for two weeks when I came down with measles. When Dr. Bloom walked through the front door of my house, I looked at him and before any introductions were even made I bawled my head off. *Why weren't my parents protecting me from these guys?* I wondered.

Basically, all kids dread and despise doctors. The only positive thing one could say about them is at least they made house calls.

And all parents revered these guys. My father would call the doctor "Herr Doctor." He would do anything the doctor suggested. If Herr Doctor would have told my father to put me up on the roof for the day, my dad would have said, "I'll get the ladder, Herr Doctor. How much do I owe you?"

This guy was as powerful as the Mikado.

I went on with the process of growing up and you know what? Eventually, fewer and fewer doctors resembled Dr. Van Baaten. At one point in my early thirties, I started gauging my imminent old age after a trip to the emergency department of a hospital with my son Danny. I realized the doctor on call was younger than me.

This is incredible, I thought. *This guy's a doctor, he's been where Dr. Van Baaten and Dr. Bloom have been, but he's younger than me. And he's wearing jeans. I'd better check to see if he has a medical degree.*

Not only was he younger than me and did not resemble Mengele, but he even spoke to my kid and he smiled. When he wanted to look into Danny's throat, he held the closed flashlight in front of Danny and asked him to blow on it in order to open the light. Danny played along and the exam was hassle-free.

Thirty years earlier in order to get me to open my mouth the Boys from Brazil would have pinched my nose and threaten to throw my Teddy bear out the third-story window.

I couldn't imagine telling Dr. Van Baaten, "Put your flashlight near my mouth. I want to blow on it to turn it on." The guy would have had me certified. And my dad would have said, "Sorry, Herr Doctor, he didn't mean it. He's a good boy really. Don't put him to sleep."

THE DEAL

And what is it that makes doctors so special? It's the fact they know more about ourselves, our bodies, than we do. I know I have a pancreas somewhere in my tummy, but I wouldn't recognize one on the street. Same thing with a fibula or an epiglottis.

When we're in pain or someone suffers an accident, the cry is, "Get a doctor!" The only exception seems to be when a hockey player gets injured. There he is writhing in pain on the ice, the other players and the referee smothering him, and who comes onto the ice to render assistance? The trainer. I never understood this one. If it were me lying there on the ice after being almost impaled by an offending hockey stick, I'd want the services of a doctor, not some guy in white baker's trousers who'll take me through the twenty-minute workout.

Doctors must really be proud of themselves, of their relevance and importance at all times and places. I am talking of medical doctors, of course. Not Ph.D.s or other D's. Although these latter people can perhaps also be proud of themselves, they're a little more expendable in society.

If someone were to have a heart attack at a shopping plaza and the cry of "Is there a doctor around?" went out, it wouldn't help if someone like Dr. Ruth was at the Baskin-Robbins around the corner. The poor victim would need some CPR, not someone saying to him, "Lie still and don't get aroused. By the way, did you ever notice an ice cream cone is a phallic symbol?"

The word "doctor" has become synonymous with the concept that if you bring your problems here, the doctor will fix them. Hence a perusal through the local telephone directory finds a sprinkling of the metaphor in the form of Dr. Copy, Dr. Deli, Dr. Roof, Dr. Pipes, Dr. Driveway, and Dr. Submarine. There is also a Fax Doctor and a Piano Doctor.

Aren't these guys about the first you'd call if you needed help from fixing a driveway to fixing you a submarine?

But then again there is even a stronger metaphor to represent medical excellence and brilliancy. We will hear people looking at some poor slug and saying, "He'll never be a brain surgeon." This is probably the *crème de la crème* of doctors, at least in the minds of the public. You never hear anyone saying, "He'll never be a dermatologist." And yet the dermatologist probably has more contact with and helps almost all of us sooner or later. Most of us will probably never go near a brain surgeon. The closest we might come this high is Dr. Roof.

HISTORY

I even considered studying medicine until that day in 1967 at Montreal's Expo 67. I had been a tour guide on the site taking visitors to different areas, including the Man and His Health pavilion, which I vividly described as featuring a film depicting open heart surgery. I flippantly mentioned that more than a hundred visitors per day pass out while watching the film. These poor visitors were caught by students earning a good wage of two dollars and seventy-five cents per hour. (It was good then; I was only getting two-fifty.)

One day I decided to walk my talk and to see the film myself. Although I had survived the vignette about the caesarian operation okay, thirty seconds into the heart movie I felt like my head, not the rest of me, was going into the Man and Outer Space Pavilion. My last words were, "I think I'll go to law school instead." Those guys earned their two dollars and seventy-five cents.

MORE HISTORY

Over the centuries there were always a group of people in the darkest of ages whose interest in Latin phrases transgressed the likes of *Et tu, Brute.* These people had the courage and the guts to look and see what was inside the human body and to wonder what made it tick. I am talking medical minds from Hippocrates to Maimonides to Harvey (the man responsible for discovering and propounding the theory of blood circulation, not some Canadian hamburger tycoon).

Considering the fact in those dark ages people often averaged a ripe old age of thirty or forty, it's amazing actually how the human race made it into the twentieth century at all.

The Black Death, for example, often wiped out entire villages. Small pox and diphtheria and cholera also took their toll during their time.

Interestingly enough I have never heard of anyone in history ever dying of a heart attack. Didn't anyone drink or smoke or eat too much? Henry VIII lived his life as a total glutton, but he didn't die because of his ticker. He died of consumption. I'm surprised none of his wives poisoned him. They probably waited for him to die of a heart attack.

Everyone else was either assassinated or they died from "the fever." Neither leeches nor bloodletting could save them.

Even in this century mortality rates were not the most promising in rural areas. I once went blueberry picking next to a cemetery in the Laurentian Mountains in Quebec. After I had picked my quota, curiosity got the better of me and I jumped over the fence to examine the gravestones. I noticed a number of stones reading something like, Lucien Beauvais, 1931–1933.

Years later I chatted with an old-timer in the area, and he told me he had twelve children originally, but six had died. He related this to me while he was puffing at his pipe, with the nonchalance of someone who would say, "Played at a badminton tournament last week. My record was six-six."

I was amazed at the casualness of Monsieur Beauvais.

Unfortunately, Canadian politicians are constantly under funding the health care system, thereby discouraging many of our physicians and enticing them to relocate to Texas where they quadruple their incomes. Damn it, Jim, we need these guys here. They're not needed at the Alamo.

THE SCHOOL

We usually place all our implicit trust in doctors because we know they have attended medical school for a number of years and have passed the requisite exams. When you see the shingle on the door and the medical degree on the wall, you say to yourself, "This guy's okay. He'll know what that pain in my abdomen is all about." The patient usually feels even more reassured if there's a bit of Latin in the diploma.

But will the doctor diagnose the problem correctly? That degree only means during the course of four years or whatever the doctor passed his exams. But by how much did he pass them? What if he got a sixty-five? What thirty-five percent didn't he know?

I know from my own experience in law school there were some things I knew better than others. I only scored a fifty in admiralty or boat law. I hated the stuff. So far after twenty-two years of practice I've managed to keep the secret safe and not misadvise a single client. But then again I never had a client walk into my downtown Toronto office and tell me he was minding his business paddling his canoe in downtown Toronto, down Bay Street about to cross Queen Street, when suddenly and without warning he was struck by the *Pacific Princess*. If it were to happen I guess I'd have to wing it.

But what about a doctor? I never asked my doctor how he did on his exams. What if he hated studying about the ear? Maybe he failed the test on ears but got through med school with flying colors because he aced other courses—maybe he got a ninety-eight on the rectum. I guess I'll never know for sure unless one day I come to him complaining about an ear ache and he tells me to pull down my pants and bend over. That would get me suspicious. I'd ask to see his report card.

HEAL ME, BABY

At one point doctors take the Hippocratic oath requiring them to heal everyone in sight. This is why

I was taken somewhat aback a few years ago when I was invited by a group of doctors to play some touch football one afternoon. There was about a dozen of them and I guess they needed one more player so they figured they would settle for a lawyer. It was only for the afternoon.

The group included an assortment of MDs including a shrink, a couple of GPs, surgeons, and internists. If you were going to get hurt, this was the time. The place looked like the set of *MASH*. I almost felt like feigning an injury just to see all the attention I might get.

Then again, I remembered I was a lawyer and I thought perhaps lawyers may not have been the most liked of professionals in times past and that just maybe, there was a loophole in Hippocrates' oath. Maybe old Hippo had once been sued for malpractice by some disgruntled patient for having left a leech in his pants. Who knows?

The game proceeded. At one point, one of the doctors touched another one a bit too zealously. Actually he tackled him. The latter, the tacklee, wasn't impressed. The other guys were asking all sorts of medical questions like, "George, are you all right?" Before brushing himself off, George responded by lunging at the tackler, a pediatrician. The two scuffled on the ground for a minute or two. I was initially shocked and then baffled. I didn't know what to make of it.

Even in times of war, doctors don't shoot at the enemy. Not only that, but they're even required to treat a wounded member of the opposition. At least I'll bet there is something in some Swiss Convention to this effect. Interestingly enough, the Swiss never go to war and yet they have all these conventions about war. It's like Gandhi being the president of the World Wrestling Federation.

So what were these doctors trying to achieve now? Was George the GP trying to do damage to his assailant Norman the pediatrician? And if he would hurt him, would he then immediately turn to examining him and try to help him?

GEORGE: Let me have a look at that sore jaw, Norman. Can you open your mouth? How did it happen?

NORMAN: Stay away, or I'll give you a mumps shot.

I enjoyed watching. So did the psychiatrist, even though he was the only one who didn't say a word. And it was his brother who got tackled. Which brings me to . . .

THE SHRINK

The thing that amazes me most about psychiatrists is that unlike other doctors, or unlike any other people, they can appear to take your money without giving you any service whatsoever.

Oh, I know lawyers are often the beneficiaries of this distinction. But you know what I mean. A family physician will tell you how to kill a flu bug. A dermatologist will always come up with some magic cream. A surgeon will fix something.

But the shrink? He'll just sit there for close to an hour. Or at least he has that option. You'd never know if he's listening to you. Or if he's even a shrink. There is always the chance he could plant an understudy in his office, anybody, who can wear a suit and sit on a chair pensively listening to your problems. You or I could be that understudy. But no way would we be able to fake it as an obstetrician. The best I could do in an emergency is say, "Quickly, bring the boiling water."

The only other occupation I can think of that anyone could fake and yet perform is that of a clown. Dressed as a clown, you can act any way under the sun and passersby will agree it's consistent with your clown identity. If you're outrageously silly, then hey, you're a clown. If you look sad and depressed, then hey, clowns are supposed to be depressed, on the inside anyway. No behavior a clown would engage in would be surprising. Now tell me a clown doesn't remind you of a shrink.

And the shrink doesn't even have to wear a rubber nose. It's optional.

NEXT

Doctors have one major fault, although they may not perceive it as such. They all keep us waiting—regardless if you're a man or woman. I don't know whether it's a ritual, a universal habit, or what, but it drives me batty. When I go to a doctor worried about the worst, I don't want to be kept waiting for an hour before I'm told I'm a hypochondriac.

I've always wondered about the reason for this waiting ritual. Is it a routine taught universally in medical schools? Is there a specific course, something like, "Waiting one-o-one?" Or do doctors take an oath to keep patients waiting?

What would happen if an undercover agent attended med school for a while to try and determine the origin of this annoying practice? The agent's secret journal of his adventures might read something like this:

September 14

I posed as a medical student, attending classes at random.

For starters I attended the opening lecture for first-year medical students, joining about 350 future white coats in the main auditorium. Interestingly enough, the class scheduled for 10:00 A.M. did not start until 10:40 A.M.. The professor walked into the hall to a cacophony of class grumbling and told the students they just had their first lesson in practical medicine. I felt I was onto something.

September 17

I returned a while later to sneak into an anatomy class in hopes of finding my answer. I had difficulty finding the anatomy hall in the basement maze and accordingly I arrived what I thought was fifteen minutes late. I dashed through the hall doors expecting to come upon the anatomy prof dissecting the unfortunate cadaver in front of a captivating audience. Instead all I saw was the subject lying on a slab with no one else in the cavernous room except another student, a philosophy student who had accidentally strayed into the wrong building expecting a lecture in Platonic metaphysics. He was not convinced he was in the wrong school; he thought the professor was the guy on the slab.

The med students and the professor (the real one) joined us about five minutes later. I waited for the professor to lift his scalpel and start cutting into the subject but instead he simply addressed his students saying, "Not bad; you kept the patient waiting twenty minutes. We'll be trying it soon with a live one."

I was getting warmer.

September 19

Following the notion that theory must precede clinical practice I thought my next stop should be the library. I was certain there was some obscure article in the medical literature about the therapeutic benefits of keeping patients waiting, although I did not quite expect any doctor ever won a Nobel prize for it.

There was a sign in front of the library: Medical Students Only.

Although I was wearing a white lab coat, I did not want to take a chance and have the security guard suspect me and so in shooting through the turnstile I commented to him, "You look a bit pale today, sir."

Unfortunately, he tried to engage me in further conversation in the hope of getting a quickie consultation. I had to think fast, act like a doctor. I told him, "I'll look at you; just wait a few minutes please." This comment put his mind to rest. A passing senior med student whispered, "Good stuff; keep him waiting." Yes indeed, I was cooking with gas (not medically speaking).

In the library I scanned the catalogues zeroing in on the history of medicine. I looked under the letter "W" hoping to catch the heading "waiting" but the closest I came was "warts."

I then scanned through names of famous physicians including Hippocrates. No luck. In fact, there were a few colorful photographs of Hippocrates' clinic depicting the great physician setting loose some leaches on a patient's back. But the pictures did not show anyone waiting in the reception area. The captions however did offer a clue. One of them read: "Hippocrates, circa 395 B.C., before the days of anesthetics, antibiotics, and waiting rooms."

I fast forwarded to the middle ages—to the 1100s and bingo! A picture of the great medieval healer Maimonides trying to keep a safe distance from a pockmarked patient with twenty other similarly pockmarked souls in an adjoining room.

In the room was a receptionist pointing to the patients with the caption reading, "The doctor is very busy today. Now who has number twenty-one?"

The picture was entitled, "Maimonides. It won't be much longer." Ah ha!!

I flipped ahead until I got to fourteenth century England. Lo and behold, there was an excerpt of one of the lesser-known of Chaucer's **Canterbury Tales** *called "The Doctour's Tayle." It starts off with a patient complaining, "Damn it, I'm not waiting any more for that quack. A plague on him."*

It is obvious the roots of modern medicine were firmly entrenched in the Middle Ages.

September 26

It occurred to me there was one exception to the waiting rule and this is at the psychiatrist's office. A shrink is almost obsessive about keeping his next appointment on time. Why?

I looked through the school schedule and noticed a psychiatry class commencing in about five minutes. I darted out of the library and arrived at the class with about two minutes to spare. Only the psychiatry professor was in the class at that time. As I was about to take my seat he told me I was two minutes early. He suggested I was anxious and compulsive and told me to wait outside. I was going to tell him he was crazy, but I was too busy trying to shrug that library security guard off my shoulder, as he was pursuing me for that consultation.

I had had enough. I told the guard his ruddy color had returned and that in any event I was just dropping out of medical school. "Too much waiting around," I told him.

October 3

Like the mysteries of the Bermuda Triangle mortals may never understand the mystery of waiting for doctors. Perhaps some puzzles are best left unsolved. For now, I will do the best I can under the circumstances. I am going off to the nearby corner store and I am buying myself an apple.

This ends mission impossible.

I will still go on thinking about the mystery next time I am cooling my heels in the comfort of my doctor's waiting room.

CHAPTER SIX

BUT IS HE A REAL DENTIST?

PAINLESS...

Unlike doctors, dentists always cause pain. This is the third certainty in life, after death and taxes. Some doctors hurt you some of the time. Psychiatrists never even touch you, or at least they shouldn't unless you perhaps tackle one in a game of touch football. A dentist, however, is guaranteed to hurt you, unless all he or she does while you sit on the chair is talk. And even this is usually painful.

And I feel they enjoy doing it. The reason is because they don't get as much respect as physicians. Whenever they introduce themselves as "Dr. So-and-So," most people ask, "What kind of doctor are you?" When the tooth person replies, "I'm a dentist," the response is usually, "Oh." The dentist doesn't have to be too perceptive to realize the questioner is saying to himself, "This guy isn't a real doctor."

And this is why they fix us when they get us in the chair.

I try to respect my dentist a hundred percent to stay exempt from punishment. I am always praising his nimble hands, comparing them to the likes of Rodin. And last time he told me he studied anatomy along with the medical students, although he concentrated primarily on the head. I said, "Hey doctor, the head is the most important part. Aren't those med students vain and picky wasting their time with the rest of the body?"

My words did not go unrewarded as this time my dentist gave me a shot of novocaine. You've got to know your human relations.

LOOK MA, NO CAVITIES

Yes, I am talking about that Crest commercial of the 1960s. The one with the little boy of about six or seven who runs into the house with a report in his hand shouting ecstatically, "Look ma, no cavities!" I always wondered, how did he get that report?

His mother is at home, there is no sign of the father, who is probably at work. Did the kid just go to the dentist's office by himself? What kid would? He might have good teeth but he'd have to be crazy. There is a greater chance of Granny going to the wolf's house to bake him a batch of muffins.

Or maybe there was some pervert standing by the school asking to look into children's mouths and then handing them certificates. We'll never know. If I had time on my hands now, I would ask the governmental department of Corporate and Consumer Affairs to launch an official investigation into the mystery. Does anybody know what became of that kid? If he can't be found, there is one reason and one reason only. He's wearing dentures.

THE DENTAL CRUSADES

My younger son Gabriel recently brought a note from school indicating a dentist will be visiting the school soon and examining the teeth of the kids in his classroom. When I called his teacher for additional information, I was told the school board was blitzing the schools with dentists in a crusade against cavities.

When I heard the word crusade, my mind suddenly went back about nine hundred years and I imagined reading the following out of a history book:

The Church and the Tooth

Little is known about the dental crusades.

In or about the year 1000, the world was in its dark age. No Renaissance, nothing. But the practice of dentistry was flourishing in western Europe. If one followed prescribed dental practices, the average person had an expectancy of keeping all his teeth for ten, maybe fifteen years.

Meanwhile in the Holy Land, tooth care was virtually unknown. The great medieval Italian dentist, Dr. Antonio de Drillo, (whom dentistry hasn't forgotten by naming an indispensable tool of the trade after him, namely, the toothbrush), wrote "Day a ruin de teeth because day eat a too much baklava . . .. You know de baklava, de cake dat's as flat as de world." Dr. de Drillo was also a prominent medieval astronomer.

The Holy Land at the time was ruled by the fierce and bellicose Turks, who in fact did not practice dental care but banned it altogether, issuing an edict that anyone caught dental flossing would be publicly whipped with his own floss. This infuriated Pope Innocent whose nephew Yakov Ben Abraham was a dentist in Nazareth.

One thing led to another and in 1087 A.D., a group of dentists met with the Pope at Clermont in France. The meeting resulted in a resolution to launch a crusade to the Holy Land in order to bring dental care to the infidels.

Their motto was "No more holes in the Holy Land." Whoever said dentists don't have a sense of humor?

Dr. de Drillo then put a filling into one of the Pope's teeth, whereupon he was promptly excommunicated; his bill was too high!

The dentists had to decide on what to wear as a symbol of their crusade. In accordance with the wishes of His Holiness, they agreed on a blue cross to be sewn on the front of their dental tunics. The cross, of course, represented the church and the blue represented the sky, the height of which Pope Innocent used to describe the current dental fees. Who ever said Popes don't have a sense of humor?

The crusade was to have left in December of 1087, but it did not get going until May of 1088 as most of the dentists were on vacation. The Pope was annoyed by the delay. He sent messages to all of their offices, but their secretaries said they were on vacation, and if he needed treatment he ought to go the local barber.

The first crusade was led by that great English dentist, Peter Plier, D.D.S. (whom dentistry also hasn't forgotten by naming another indispensable tool of the trade after him, namely, the drill).

The trip to the Holy Land was not without complications, as many of the dentists never made it past the Swiss Alps; they loved Switzerland so much they decided to stay.

Others had difficulties on the seas, their ships being attacked by pirates who would steal all of the silver fillings and use them for stud earrings. One ship of dentists mysteriously vanished, and it is believed to have drifted to the New World, probably Massachusetts. No one knows for sure, but to this day there is a village on Cape Cod where all the inhabitants have this inexplicable obsession to wash their hands constantly and say, "Open wide."

When the crusading dentists finally made it to the Holy Land, they were met with fierce opposition. They besieged the City of Jerusalem and they did not let anyone in or out of the walled city without an appointment. This proved to be too much for the inhabitants and after several weeks the city fell to the dentists.

The crusaders did not stop there. They captured city after city and set up dental clinics throughout the Holy Land. The blue cross was everywhere.

The clinics were not fancy. The consisted of just a simple dental chair or two, surrounded by a massive crusader's fortress to prevent gate crashing. Each clinic would have a dentist, one or two secretaries, and two burly dental assistants to chain the patient down. Tooth freezing had not yet been perfected. The odd clinic also employed a dental hygienist to hum.

One of the leading dentists was Paul The Painless of York. He was known as the father of orthodontia, having developed various braces for crooked teeth. The braces were crude, but then again, what would you expect in 1089 A.D.?

Paul's experiments eventually led to his demise. One day his right index finger got stuck in a brace he had just fitted into the mouth of one of Sultan Saladin's teenage wives, Salama. It was impossible to remove either the finger or the brace and after about two weeks, Saladin lost his patience and took drastic action, banishing both Painless and Salama from the Holy Land. Whoever said Saladin didn't have a sense of humor?

After a few years, the idealism of the dental crusaders waned and they started feuding among themselves. They would sabotage one another's clinics by booking appointments and not showing up. This would infuriate the secretaries who would respond by insulting and abusing the next patient who just happened to be walking in.

Many dentists simply became homesick for the amenities of home, including their friends and families, home cooking, the bubonic plague, etc.

Not surprisingly, most of the dentists returned home. And so ended the dental crusade.

Actually, there was a second but ill-fated and short-lived crusade in the year 1188 called the Children's Crusade.

This involved thousands of European children who planned to march from Europe to the Holy Land to hand out toothbrushes and pamphlets on dental hygiene to local children. Unfortunately, they never made it as the Turks intercepted them at

Constantinople and convinced them to return to Europe by giving them large bags of jelly beans.

I don't know whether this is exactly what my kid's school principal meant, but to me a crusade is serious business.

IS THERE A DENTIST IN THE BASEMENT?

I didn't go to a real dentist until my mid teens. Let me explain. After World War II, there was a wave of immigration to Canada and with the wave came people who claimed to have been different things in eastern Europe. Some claimed to have practiced dentistry there. Whereas some may indeed have been legitimate dentists, others were dental technicians, who spent their time making false teeth. When they moved to Canada they decided to give it a go as dentists. Neither the real ones nor the optimists were licensed to practice in Canada. All worked underground. Which brings me to Dr. Neustein.

He was a Romanian gentleman who worked out of a basement in downtown Montreal. My parents used to take me there whenever I had a toothache. Many of our friends and family went there. I imagine he didn't charge as much as the real dentists.

Dr. Neustein obviously had some knowledge about teeth, having a fine set of gold teeth in his own mouth. He scared me actually, reminding me in retrospect of that James Bond character, "Jaws."

I really doubt whether or not he ever spent a day in dental school, although my parents still accorded him the address, "Herr Doctor." This address in itself meant imminent pain for me. My kids today call their dentist Brian.

You'd ring his doorbell and his wife would look suspiciously through the curtain, let you in, and lead you down a steep staircase into the basement. There rested a chair which certainly resembled a dental chair, perhaps of the 1930s. I am sure that after Dr. Neustein retired from practice, the chair and attached torture equipment were acquired by the movie studio for use in the scene from *Marathon Man*. I am referring to the scene where Lawrence Olivier, who plays a former Nazi butcher, the White Angel, starts drilling indiscriminately into Dustin Hoffman's teeth, trying to elicit information.

Neustein would poke around with his probe and then start drilling randomly, without anesthetic of course. The drill moved so slowly I have no doubt Mrs. Neustein was standing nearby turning a hand crank. At least that's probably what he was telling her in Romanian to do, while I was sharing Dustin Hoffman's fate. I didn't care much for her either. All she ever said in English was "nice boy." I felt like Hansel. If she had her knitting with her she would have been a dead ringer for a Romanian Madame Defarge.

Every couple of minutes when I asked for a time out the White Angel would stop the inquisition and say, "Rinse pliss."

When I insisted he do something about the pain, he offered to drill a little slower. He said that would help. When I sat back down for the next inning, the pain was the same and I was out of there. My father would say, "You have to let Dr. Neustein work on you or you'll get a toothache." In case I haven't mentioned it before, my father did not spend his life in sales or public relations.

Unlike the "dentists" I frequented in later years, Dr. Neustein charged by the tooth. Three dollars per filling per tooth, regardless of the work done. The real McCoys charged by the "surface." And each tooth has a couple of surfaces. It was, therefore, in my father's best interest that when I developed cavities, these cavities be concentrated in one tooth and the business not be spread around to its neighbors.

All hell broke loose one day after I complained of a toothache, and Dr. N asked for six bucks. Jaws insisted he worked on two teeth and my father insisted it was only one toothache. Dr. Neustein asked me to sit down again and open my mouth to enable him to explain some dental anatomy to my doubting dad. I felt like a witness being cross-examined in a courtroom.

They each took turns making me open my mouth and pointing to different teeth while they shouted at one another. Even Mrs. Neustein got into the picture opening my mouth once or twice and poking around with her fingers, in full support of her husband's position.

When my father started questioning this guy's credentials, Dr. N claimed he was once the personal dentist for King Michael, the former king of Romania. My father replied, "You mean King Michael the Toothless?"

The vigorous debate ended when, upon re-examination by Dr. Neustein in a further effort to persuade my father, his fingers went into my mouth a bit too deeply. I reacted by giving him a good bite, breaking the skin on his index finger. It was one of my greatest moments in life when I saw him wince in pain. This moment was matched only by my watching that scene in *Marathon Man* where the White Angel gets bumped off.

Dr. Neustein shouted at me, calling me "crazy boy."

I responded saying, "Rinse pliss."

In the midst of the confusion while Mrs. Neustein tended to her husband's wounded finger, my dad and I took off like Butch Cassidy and the Sundance Kid.

I guess this was not the best time to ask Dr. Neustein if he could give me one of those no cavity reports.

CHAPTER SEVEN

LAW, NOT A NOTE THAT FOLLOWS SO

AN APPLE A DAY . . . DOES NOTHING FOR LAWYERS

I know exactly why I became a lawyer. Back in seventh grade my teacher and I did not get along too well and Mr. Goldstein abruptly ended our daily debates by kicking me out of class.

He would say with unparalleled eloquence, "Get out."

I made a notch on the wall outside for each trip and the total at the end of the year was 133. The Toronto Maple Leafs should only score that well.

Although some acts of excommunication by Mr. Goldstein were properly in order, most weren't justified, and this was simply his way of getting rid of the problem.

I found myself often saying to him, "This isn't justice."

His enlightened response was, "I said get out."

Over the months I developed this desire to ensure that justice was done, at least occasionally. I thought of a few career options. I had not done too much thinking by that time about the future, although the most appealing job to me at the time was streetcar driver. I loved the idea of punching transfers, making change, dealing with the public, and driving that great big toy. Now I had to ask myself whether my new goal of achieving justice could be attained in this occupation.

While it would be fun to operate a trolley and deal with the public, once again I did not visualize my potential supervisor standing at the terminal when I bring the streetcar in after a run and saying to me, "Right has prevailed."

And anyway, at that time the Montreal Transportation Commission started phasing out streetcars in favor of gas-guzzling buses.

By the time I was twelve I had never met a lawyer in person. The necessity of visiting a lawyer did not quite rival that of visiting a dentist. Although, on second thought, by that age I probably had never met a real dentist either. Who knows what Dr. Neustein was!

Nor had I cause to be inside a courtroom. My only exposure to the world of law was watching episodes of Perry Mason.

You will note most movies involving lawyers and trials deal with murder cases. *To Kill a Mockingbird, Witness for the Prosecution, Obsession*—to name a few. And every Perry Mason episode I could remember involved a murder trial. Not one show extolled the excitement of incorporating a company.

Naturally I presumed that's about all lawyers do, namely defend people innocently accused of murder. And now after twenty-plus years of practicing law, I have yet to come face to face with a real murderer. I never seem to meet the real ones.

I have also had some time to reflect carefully upon Perry Mason's illustrious career.

POOR PERRY MASON

After careful analysis I have come to the conclusion my childhood idol Perry Mason probably ended up an obscure bankrupt.

I recently watched another couple of rerun episodes, in between heated discussions with my bank manager, and I am convinced beyond a reasonable doubt that Perry Mason must have gone belly up unless he supplemented his law practice income by driving taxi.

The telltale signs of a law practice in trouble were obvious in the very first scene of the counselor's office. It was readily apparent Mason's entire practice consisted of one active case. Can anyone say they ever saw any files on his desk?

In fact, the only paper in the office was supplied by his secretary, Della Street, in the form of her steno pad when she was summoned by Perry to record the interview with the unfortunate client. The client would admit it looked bad for her, but insisted she was innocent notwithstanding the fact the police found her fingerprints on the poker which bludgeoned the deceased.

At least his office wasn't too pretentious. I note he didn't even have a swivel chair, making do with a simple low back wooden seat. He was often seen sitting on the front corner of his desk as he chatted with his client. I imagine this was made possible only by the fact his desk remained uncluttered by files.

I would have expected that legal wiz to be inundated with clients, not because he was invincible but because he never asked his clients for a deposit retainer. I have watched dozens of shows and I am still waiting for him to say, "I'll need five hundred dollars up front." (This was the 1950s, after all.) Maybe if he would have gotten paid he would have been able to afford a better chair.

But if his lot was so bad, what can we say about the plight of Hamilton Burger, the District Attorney? We don't doubt he got paid, although probably not too much. You will note he always wore that same light gray suit.

And what a life! We all win some and lose some, but Hamilton never won a case. I have watched him in action carefully trying to analyze his technique in an attempt to account for his dismal record of no wins and about seven thousand losses.

It's amazing what you can get away with working as a civil servant! If he were to display this type of bleak track record in private practice, after three months his partners would have him to doing research.

Yet, if you think about it, Burger's demeanor readily matched Perry's. His "objection, Your Honor," was just as sound as Perry Mason's, but it was all to no avail. I can only conclude the fault lay not with Hamilton Burger but rather with Lieutenant Tragg, the crusty old detective who accounted for all the arrests on the show.

In view of the fact Perry Mason got everyone of the defendants off, has anyone ever realized that Tragg must have arrested thousands of innocent people? He has to be history's worst cop. He always arrested the wrong person and then he handed the lemon of a case over to Hamilton Burger who then got tagged for the loss. Sending Burger into court with a Lieutenant Tragg arrest was about as fair as sending Wayne Gretzky onto the ice without a jock strap.

But still, what made the great Perry Mason tick?

One thing I noticed is Della was always in court at his counsel table with her ubiquitous steno pad glued to her hand. Considering Perry only had one client I guess it did not matter what Della was doing. But what happened if she was in court and the phone would ring? This was before the days of the answering machine. Nor did I ever hear an answering service get Mason's line. No wonder he only had one client. He was unreachable!

But the quality that set Perry Mason leagues above other lawyers was his never-ending ability not only to secure acquittals for his clients but also to apprehend the actual murderer. He would do this to the amazement of Lieutenant Tragg and Hamilton Burger.

For some inexplicable reason, at every murder trial the real murderer always seemed to attend the trial of the innocent accused. He was just asking for it, like the male courting the female spider. Invariably at the end of the episode, investigator Paul Drake walked in, whispered something to Mason and a minute later the murderer stood up in the courtroom and said, "Okay, I did it. It was my poker."

After hundreds of cases Hamilton Burger and Lieutenant Tragg should have realized the trick was to start with the trial, seal off the courtroom—prohibiting anybody from leaving—and then interrogate all the spectators. This technique worked wonders for Charlie Chan. Dollars to donuts says the murderer would be in the courtroom. The concept of leaving town just never occurred to the rogues in Perry Mason stories. They always came back, like a spawning salmon.

Although Perry Mason probably never made any money out of practicing law (no doubt being the prototype of lawyers of the nineties), the California taxpayer must have saved a fortune. With Perry Mason securing not only all those acquittals but also the concomitant confessions of the real culprits, the California Court of Appeals was probably about as busy as the Maytag repairman.

TINKER, TAILOR, OR INDIAN CHIEF

I was not sure by the time I got to the university I was even suited for law school. I took a battery of vocational tests, the multiple-choice type, given by a vocational psychologist to help me determine what career path to follow. There were questions like, "Would you rather invent the car, design the car, advertise the car, sell the car, fix the car . . .?" You get the idea. Nowhere was there an option, "Represent someone who was run over by the car."

It's no wonder in a test tending to show my interest in an occupation, out of a list of one hundred careers, lawyer ranked seventy-two. Number two was musician. I had never played an instrument in my life. Number one was funeral director. Perhaps something about my sense of humor. Who knows?

One thing positive came out of all this testing. I eliminated from my possible choice a career as a vocational psychologist.

LAW SCHOOL

If there is anything any law student remembers from law school it's two words: "reasonable man." In trying to determine whether or not a party was negligent, the test is whether he acted like the "reasonable man on the Clapham Street omnibus." This was some municipal bus line in London, England, no doubt. Perhaps American law students call him the reasonable man on the Hyde and Powell Street cable car. Or the IRT 7th Avenue Line. Or the BART. I can go on, but I am sure you get the idea.

This guy's supposed to be your Mr. Average. He is not overly cautious, yet he is prudent enough to go out after a bout of freezing rain and dump a shovel of salt on his frosty walk so that reasonable people visiting him later on don't slip and fall and break a reasonable leg.

He's supposed to make sure his dog won't bite you, but within reason. If he owns a pit bull terrier, he is expected to be on his guard more than if his pooch is a cocker spaniel. If however his cocker spaniel takes a nibble off the mailman, then the question is did Mr. defendant act like the reasonable man on the Clapham Street omnibus? (Or the El in Chicago?)

What would he have done under the circumstances?

Try telling your client, who is being sued for fifty thousand dollars, "Sir, the judge will try to determine

119

whether you acted reasonably, like the reasonable man on the Clapham Street omnibus."

The not unexpected response will be, "Huh?"

You see nobody has ever met this phantom rider. Even if he exists, I'll bet he doesn't own a cocker spaniel. If he did, he'd probably buy it for his kids because it's reputed to be docile and friendly.

This is why my client who was sued bought Figaro, the doggie who took a dislike to the pizza delivery man.

So now we're wondering what Mr. Clapham would have done to prevent his spaniel from taking an advance on the pizza.

Well, there is no Santa Claus. There is no reasonable man on the Clapham omnibus, even presuming this route in merry old England still exists decades after it was first referred to by some British law lord and hallowed in our legal system.

It all gets down to this. I won my case. I won not because what that gentleman on the bus would have done. We all know hindsight is twenty-twenty. I won because in giving his judgment, His Honor commented on the fact he as a lad owned a cocker spaniel. "Ginger was the kindest creature on four legs," said His Honor. He suggested it was inconceivable how a dog such as Figaro could lunge at the plaintiff without sufficient provocation. He found there must have been incitement by the pizza man, and the judge dismissed the case.

Although happy, I couldn't for the life of me figure out what kind of provocation His Honor had in mind. The pizza man just stepped through the door and said, "Hi." He wasn't even late.

On the other hand, it wasn't really my client's fault. He was as shocked as the pizza guy. Not as hurt, just as shocked. He didn't even eat the pizza that night.

I asked myself at the conclusion of the trial, was justice done? I don't know. You'd have to ask the reasonable man on the Clapham Street omnibus.

THE QUESTION

A quick test. What is the question lawyers are asked most frequently? Clue. It has nothing to do with money.

Time's up. Answer: How can you defend someone knowing he's guilty?

The answer. None of my clients are ever guilty or at fault for that matter. They always tell me they're right and from the sound of it they are.

HE'S A REAL NOWHERE MAN

I frequently hear the woes of clients describing a fender bender where they insist they are totally blameless. They often use an expression of innocence which asserts their exemplary driving but on the other hand leaves the listener totally baffled as to how the accident possibly could have taken place.

The saintly party usually says: "I looked both ways before entering the intersection. The coast was clear and suddenly bang, this guy came out of nowhere."

As a lawyer I usually ask innocently, "But surely he had to come out of somewhere?"

"No, he wasn't there when I looked. I tell you he just came out of nowhere," replies "Mother Theresa."

As I have experienced a number of similar complaints over the years, I have to ask where indeed do these scoundrels come from just when the innocent driver feels it's safe to proceed, only to be totaled by this sudden force. Is there a "nowhere"? I have given this matter some thought.

I looked at Webster's Dictionary, which defines nowhere as "a place that does not exist." At first blush it appears there is no way these phantom cars can come out of nowhere, as nowhere is nowhere to be found. It simply does not exist. The good dictionary goes on to cite examples of how the word has been used in literature and it contains a quote by author Bill Wolf: "The lumbermen, construction workers, and miners who are carving towns out of nowhere in Canada . . ."

Is it possible therefore that nowhere exists, but only in Canada? Like the Royal Canadian Mounted Police? Is it in Manitoba, near Winnepeg?

The question then becomes how do these mystery drivers appear on the scene almost instantaneously to do their damage?

One possibility is what I will call the Star Trek theory. You will recall Scotty used to beam people to and from the starship *Enterprise.*

What if there is a similar force at work beaming cars and making them appear suddenly in front of unsuspecting motorists?

Don't knock this suggestion. People laughed at Jules Verne a century ago when he fantasized about moon trips. Maybe one day instead of charging the poor soul who looks carefully both ways only to get hit by the man from nowhere, the police will write out a summons to Captain Kirk. Maybe he's the one who engineers the beamings.

I was in fact about to endorse this theory personally when something happened to make me consider other possibilities.

My wife was driving to a nearby mall when suddenly a gentleman in a spiffy sports car shot out from the mall exit and broadsided our vehicle. The investigating officer interrogated both my wife and "Mario Andretti." When asked for an explanation, Mario said he looked both ways and when he saw no one in sight, he released his foot off the brake, gently rolling into the main street, only to hit our car which came out of "nowhere."

After my wife related the story, I queried, "Before the accident, were you on a space ship with Vulcans aboard?"

She looked at me and put her hand on my forehead to check for fever.

I persisted questioning to determine from whence she came just prior to arriving at the unfortunate mall exit. Although reticent at first, the good woman broke down and confessed to coming from the nearby Dunkin Donuts. She added she would start her promised diet tomorrow.

Now I have frequented this donut place before, and it is definitely not a place that does not exist. I have the waistline to prove it.

I telephoned the policeman and he read me the other driver's statement where he said, "The road was empty. I saw *nothing* coming."

I actually found this comment disconcerting. While my wife may not have been driving a red

Porsche, I have had several good years of service from my Chevrolet Celebrity and I wouldn't call it nothing. To give the man the benefit of the doubt, I asked my wife and she denied having sprayed the vehicle before the accident with that invisible paint I have seen advertised on kiddy cartoon shows.

The officer also told me "Speedy Gonzales" insisted, "The coast was clear and there was *nobody* around."

I found this allegation preposterous as it did not take Descartes to convince me my wife existed. She was definitely not a figment of my imagination. In fact, she promptly slapped my hand as I squeezed her ear. To date, my investigation still remains inconclusive as I do not know the whereabouts of nowhere. But the quest must go on as one thing is for sure, in the foreseeable future many more vehicles will originate from there.

LET RIGHT PREVAIL—THE CHICKEN MAN

I had a case once involving a client who kept a platoon of chickens. Not on a farm but in his backyard in downtown Toronto. Aside from using the eggs, he just enjoyed his pastoral rural oasis. He also drank only spring water, bicycled to work, recycled everything. You've got it.

The house had been around about a hundred years and I know for sure my client, whom I'll call Rodney Wilks, could readily trace his ancestors back to the Duke of Wellington.

Rodney was an academic associated with the local university.

On the other side in the red corner was a Frenchman, his neighbor, Jean Claude Boulet. Monsieur Boulet grew up in downtown Paris and he enjoyed nothing more than coming home from his hair salon at the end of a hard day and lounging in his backyard patio sipping a glass of wine. He had a dog, a beagle called François.

Although you might expect the two sides naturally to get along just fine, surprisingly some friction developed. Monsieur Boulet started bugging my client. First, he complained my client's chickens were smelly. He insisted he had the right to sit on his patio without having to ingest the scent of these pullets. Now there was a Brit-hating racist if I ever saw one.

Then he insisted the birds were noisy. The constant clucking of the hens were bad enough, but the worst part was that rooster who sounded *reveille* every morning at the crack of dawn. The more he would ask my client to do something, the more Rodney would dig in deeper, insisting a man's home was his castle. Surely that Frenchman should have understood this fundamental right. Or else he should have stayed in France. Right?

Monsieur Boulet it seems counterattacked. First, he sent François to relieve himself on Rodney's bicycle. Other dogs would be content to pick trees or fire hydrants but Boulet trained that mongrel to switch to my poor client's sole means of transportation.

One thing lead to another. The final straw was the day François grabbed one of my client's chickens by his snout and carried her out of the backyard and onto the sidewalk.

No harm actually came to the hen, except for the fact she got very nervous, expecting perhaps that she was on her final destination to Kentucky Fried Chicken.

My client, in the totally defensive mood of a man defending his castle, went out with his broom and nudged François a bit. Monsieur Boulet noticing the cajoling with the broom apparently mistook the scene and he charged out and tackled my totally innocent client on the sidewalk. What ensued was Wrestlemania 12, resulting in each side charging the other with assault.

At the trial the prosecutor backed off, and it was agreed each lawyer would act as prosecutor against the other party as well as defense counsel for his own.

The evidence went on for an entire day. During the trial the other side introduced all sorts of irrelevant evidence about Rodney's chickens. Neighbors testified about the alleged smells and sounds. The other lawyer even suggested to the judge, pointing to the broom which had become "exhibit four," that my client ought to have been charged under the Criminal Code with possession of a dangerous weapon.

Rodney was no less zealous in his argument suggesting François was not a beagle at all, alleging wildly his mother was actually a pit bull terrier. This lead to further outbursts in the court by each side about the other's mother. Rodney demanded the hound be put to sleep forthwith.

The trial could have gone on longer. I had to use all my persuasive powers to get my client from bringing the victimized chicken to court. Anyway, I don't think the hen would have agree to come without a subpoena.

The trial ended with the judge throwing his hands up in the air and dismissing all charges against everyone. He suggested the parties shake hands. He may as well have suggested Wile E. Coyote shake hands with the Roadrunner.

Who was right, who was wrong? Like I started to say, my clients are never wrong. Ask Rodney Wilks.

CHOP CHOP

You are now asking the second most common question lawyers are asked. Do I support capital punishment?

The answer is I am a staunch advocate of capital punishment, as long as nobody actually gets executed. You see there's something just too final about executions that troubles me. You can't simply come back a year or two later if there is new evidence and ask for a new hearing. The best the system will give you at that stage is a sincere "oops."

But I have a great idea. I recently watched a performance of Gilbert and Sullivan's *The Mikado* in which the Lord High Executioner Koko is ordered by the Mikado to execute someone. Having never actually executed anyone to date, poor Koko's nerve fails him. When the Mikado later asks him why he did not chop off the block of a culprit as ordered, Koko replies that when the great Mikado orders something done, it is as good as done.

To paraphrase further, the actual doing of the deed is superfluous and unnecessary as the deed is deemed to have been performed after the order is uttered by the Mikado.

Now wouldn't this be a cleaner and more humane form of capital punishment than say, the electric chair? And it would even save on hydro. I believe we should legislate this bloodless form of execution everywhere.

Upon conviction for a capital offense, the presiding justice would still utter the death penalty sentence. His Honor could then choose any method of execution he pleases and he could even take suggestions from the jury. The accused would then be deemed to have been executed in that manner, subject to a ceremonial execution to follow once the period for appealing had expired.

If for instance, the justice is in the mood for a bit of French ceremony, he might order the accused, we may as well call him Mr. Brown, to be guillotined. As there would be no actual head rolling, the execution could be public to promote the cause for a general deterrence. A guillotine equipped with a rubber blade would be set up in front of the local city hall, a drum roll would sound and chop, the execution would be completed.

No doubt there would be some clown of a convict with a beard who would probably recall Sir Thomas More's chop chop execution and utter to the executioner something about ensuring his beard isn't hit in the process as said beard "hath committed no offense."

And we must not, of course, forget that special request for a favorite last meal. With a mock physical denouement, this last meal would make a lot more sense. After all, the felon would get an opportunity to digest it.

I still don't believe the stories I read about prisoners on death row in the United States who can think of nothing else prior to their final walk other than ordering something like medium-rare prime ribs, french fries, a chocolate eclair, and a six-pack of Miller Lite.

I have yet to read about the poor soul who says, "Last meal? Are you kidding? Who could think of food at a time like this?"

In imposing a sentence, the judge might order something like a Writ of Execution, certifying the accused has been executed as of a certain date. After the execution a doctor would examine the accused. Actually, I do not think this part is necessary, but the government probably needs more records and paperwork. The physician would only conduct a cursory exam, checking the man's heart and asking how he's feeling. If the guy said, "Okay," the doctor would tell him, "No you're not. You're defunct." He could take a blood pressure reading which might read, actual, 140 over 85; deemed, 0."

I've always wondered about the examinations conducted by doctors in these instances. I remember a couple of years back a photograph in the papers of a doctor taking former Romanian President Nikolai Caeucescu's blood pressure reading minutes before he and his wife were to face a firing squad. There was something very morbid about this procedure. What would the doctor have told the president if the reading came out sky high? "Nikolai, you'd better lay off that sodium."

Getting back to the unfortunate Mr. Brown, let me make one thing perfectly clear. Once deemed dead, the accused would suffer all the amenities exclusive to deceased persons. His executor would be able to probate his will. All property jointly held with his wife would vest in her. And of course he would no longer receive mail, not consistently anyway. Many of us don't have to die to be the beneficiaries of this latter service.

His pension rights would cease. He would not be able to incorporate a company, and he would not be a competent witness in any future court proceedings. As he would be totally useless, he would still, however, be eligible for appointment to the Canadian Senate.

A death certificate would issue and the fact of his expiration would be duly noted on his driver's license, thereby prohibiting him from operating a motor vehicle anywhere other than in Montreal. In that fine city, I don't think from the way people drive that anybody actually ever passed a driving test.

The advantages of this system are clear. Aside from the fact no life gets snuffed out, the process is reversible. If, for example, a convicted man's innocence is later discovered— and we have seen this happen a number of times—there would be no problem in bringing him back from the dead. His lawyers might apply for something called Returnus the Corpus. The only problem I foresee is the lawyer getting paid. The deceased could conceivably argue when he returns that he was dead when he hired the lawyer, and therefore, he had no status to enter into any legal contracts. But that's a problem for us lawyers to iron out.

I feel this method of capital punishment would placate both the proponents and abolitionists. In fact, I am so keen about the idea I shall be sending a letter immediately to my federal government representative with the proposal.

As I want to ensure he gets it promptly, of course, I won't be dropping the letter into the mailbox.

SO YOU WANT TO BE A DOCTOR OR A LAWYER?

For some reason or other these two words are often muttered together, like Tweedledum and Tweedledee. Or like St. Paul and Minneapolis. Or like Dallas and Forth Worth. Or like Wilber and Orville. You get the picture.

My parents always wanted me to pick one profession or the other. In fact, they made it seem like those were the only professions in existence. Growing up was like living in a world of Baskin-Robbins but only ever coming across vanilla and chocolate.

I indicated earlier, my first preference was becoming a streetcar driver. As the Montreal Transportation Commission removed the trams by the early 1960s, this option was out, unless I would have considered moving to San Francisco (the Powell and Hyde Street line and all that).

This left law or medicine. As I couldn't stand anything doctors did, this left law. Of the two professions, I have come to the conclusion doctors are a lot more significant to society than lawyers are, at least on a crisis per capita basis. In other words, you would never dial 911 to get a lawyer. True, if you get arrested or your spouse slaps you with a summons seeking 110 percent of your net worth, you'd rather call a lawyer. Unless the initial shock gives you a heart attack.

I once flew overseas when a flight attendant on the plane accidentally spilled some hot coffee on a passenger. After the scream, an announcement came over the P.A. requesting the assistance of any doctor. In fifteen seconds the lady had three doctors plus a nurse at her side. I felt like helping too but what could I possibly have done? Offer to draw up her will?

This inability to help in a health crisis does sometimes phase me.

Incidentally, I watched the doctors ordering the nurse around and she was complying handing them this and that. It occurred to me that she was a complete stranger to the doctors. She could have just said, "I don't even know you guys. Bug off." Amazing, the eternal power of Herr Doctor.

At least lawyers are more gracious, willing to share the glory of a great legal case with their clients. For example, any landmark case is remembered not by the lawyer but by the name of the key players. The rule in *McNaughten's* case, which deals with the century-old plea of insanity, is so-named after Mr. McNaughten. He killed someone and got away with it when his brilliant lawyer saved him from execution by propounding the principle of not guilty by reason of insanity.

Same deal with the rule in *Hedley Byrne*, which is about negligent statements. The ancient rule in *Shelley's* case, about land law, or the more recent *Askov* case, about the right under the Canadian Charter of Rights and Freedom to a speedy criminal trial.

Doctors, on the other hand, hog all the glory. The diseases are frequently named after the name of the physician who discovered a treatment. I am thinking of Crohn's disease, Parkinson's disease, Alzheimer's disease, Hodgkin's disease, to name a few. You never hear about the unfortunate patient at all. Well maybe one. But I don't think the poor sufferer was glorified by doctors calling the disease "elephant man's dis-ease."

In this way, at least lawyers humanize the pro-cess. They share something with the clients. The case isn't simply "Bed B."

UNDER THE BORDER

There are a number of misconceptions as to what actually happens in a courtroom. These myths are generated by movies and television shows. You see, things are run a little differently in Canada than they are south of the border:

Objection

No such animal here. If the lawyer doesn't like what the other lawyer is saying, generally because he's getting close to the truth, he or she will not say "objection." If he does the judge might say, "What is it, Mr. Mason?"

The drill is to stand up. When the judge sees you, he or she will say something like, "Yes, what is it Mr. Mason?"

The lawyer will then think of something impor-tant to say having successfully interrupted his adversary's train of thought and effective cross-ex-amination of the witness.

Although we don't use the word objection, it is beyond me why in Canada we have not come up with an alternate word. Something simple. How about "hello"?

Order in the court

I have been practicing in the Canadian courts for over twenty years and I have never seen a gavel in the courtroom. Yet there is not a caricature of a judge without a gavel in his hand. This again must be an American creation. I don't know what the purpose of a gavel would be in any event. The voice from the bench readily gets heard throughout. It's not as if the courtroom is the size of Yankee Stadium.

I guess the reason why the American judges have gavels is security. It may not be a magnum, but I've seen these hammers and a zealous litigant might think twice before lunging at the bench with his fingers.

Will counsel approach the bench

No such animal in Canada either. People watching from the body of the court might get the idea the judge is having a private conversation with the lawyers to their respective detriment. Also I guess one party might have better ears than the other and thereby pick up the private conversation. He could then wink at his less endowed opponent and all hell might break loose.

In Canadian courts, if the judge wants a private conversation with counsel, he recesses the court and says, "I want to see counsel in my chambers." This then really gives the litigants a good reason to feel something secretive is going on behind their backs and their respective lawyers are trying to sell them out.

This comment will be stricken from the record

Another all-American feature. And an amusing one at that. We see a lawyer suggesting to a witness charged with assault something improper and irrelevant like, "And I understand sir that you have an automatic firearm collection," and after he cries "Yes!" before the opposing lawyer gets a chance to object, he demands and the judge orders, "This testimony will be stricken from the record. The jury will disregard this evidence."

Like Dorothy said of the Scarecrow, I like this one the most. Here we have twelve people who are given the responsibility of determining whether a person goes free or possibly goes to jail or worse. Yet the judge expects them to act like morons and wilfully forget some of the juiciest testimony of the trial.

In Canadian courts nothing ever gets stricken from the record. The judge may merely remind the jurors during his final charge to the jury that they should not take this evidence into account. I am sure no Canadian jury would even think of rendering their decision with this tainted evidence when asked to disregard it.

The Queen v. The People

In the United States, the prosecution side of a criminal case is referred to as "The People." In other words the case will be designated as *The People v. Brown*. In Canada, the people are replaced collectively and substituted by "the Queen." The Latin designation is usually used and so the court docket will read, *Regina v. Brown*.

Our prosecutors are even referred to as Crown Attorneys or simply as Crowns. South of the border they're District Attorneys or DAs.

I prefer the American system as the Canadian one puts too much pressure on Her Majesty the

Queen. For example, if the culprit Mr. Brown decides to shoplift from a Wal-Mart in Dallas, then it is the people of Texas who will prosecute him. When the culprit Brown sees the docket reading *The People of Texas v. Brown*, he'll no doubt get overwhelmed and this will be the last the courts will see of him. He'll think twice before committing another larceny. All the people of Texas are certainly a massive force to face, more massive than even Wal-Mart.

But if he were to do the same thing in Edmonton, it would be Brown against the Queen. One on one. If he's any sort of chauvinist, I doubt he'll be put off by a septuagenarian lady across the ocean waiving her finger at him and saying, "Shame, shame."

Furthermore, prosecuting thousands of charges a year must put a tremendous strain on Her Majesty. Imagine the busy schedule she has performing her monarchial duties like traveling to New Guinea to watch tribal dances or attending state dinners from Ottawa to San Francisco (the Powell and Hyde Street line!). The last thing she needs is to get a call on her cellular phone from some police officer in Edmonton asking, "Your Majesty, what do you want us to do with Mr. Brown?"

Even if Wal-Mart might want the charges dropped, it is the Queen herself who is the aggrieved party, the victim so to speak. When that rogue snatched the shampoo from Wal-Mart, little did he know Her Majesty Queen Elizabeth II might have to go next door to her son Edward and say, "Excuse me. Can I borrow your Head and Shoulders?"

It would therefore only be fair for the loss to be spread among all the people as it is in the United States. Meanwhile, God Save the Queen. She needs it.

A BIGGER POCKET TO PICK

Insurance

In a personal injury case a lawyer is not supposed to mention the word insurance to a jury. The results of doing so are almost similar to what happened to that character in the Monty Python movie, *Life With Brian*. In that flick, there is a scene in an ancient Holy Land city two thousand years ago where a group of inhabitants are about to stone a man condemned to die for uttering the word, "Jehovah."

You don't dare say the word insurance. The judge even goes the other way in his charge telling the jury they should not temper their judgment in any way if they feel the defendant may not have the funds to pay any award they might order.

The legal system presumes once six men and women take their places in the jury box, they forget they drive cars and they have something called insurance premiums. Maybe the judge expects them to strike that from the record.

THE VOIRE DIRE

During the course of a criminal trial, the judge may ask the jurors to leave while he or she listens to arguments from the lawyers in a juryless courtroom. Most often the situation arises as the police have gotten the accused to admit to something and the defense lawyer would now like to keep this from the jury as the admission or confession could be enough to nail the accused. There will be arguments made about the statement being involuntary or the rights of the accused were otherwise violated (i.e. he wasn't

137

read his right to remain silent). The procedure in the absence of the jury is called a voire dire.

But the judge doesn't explain it to the jury exactly that way. He says something like, "Counsel has something to discuss with me which should be heard in the absence of the jury."

The jury members then go, "Okay, let's leave."

Now do you think most juries go out to their jury room and start playing Trivial Pursuit or bridge, saying to one another, "I wonder what that secret discussion could be about"? By now they probably all say to themselves, "Uh huh! A confession. I knew he's guilty."

Or maybe they're angry at the judge for getting the boot out, and they come back later and deliberately find the accused not guilty.

There's never a dull moment in the world of law.

Yet why are there so many days I would rather be driving that streetcar?

CHAPTER EIGHT

PEOPLE NEEDING PEOPLE

A CERTAIN INDIVIDUAL

When I was a lad of about seven I was walking along Montreal's Rue Saint Denis one day with my mother when I noticed a commotion. We found ourselves in a crowd that had gathered near the curb to stare at a poor lady who had been hit by a car while trying to cross the street. This was not an unusual occurrence for a pedestrian in Montreal.

In addition to the dozens of onlookers, two police officers who had arrived on the scene were directing traffic. Or should I say they were redirecting it, asking vehicles in either directions to back up and detour. This was okay for the cars but it made life most difficult for the streetcars. They were marooned indefinitely it seemed.

Eventually an ambulance arrived on the scene and took the lady to the hospital. At least I presume that's what it did. (Didn't it?)

What astounded me was that probably hundreds of people were caught by this poor lady's fate. They were expected to comply and lose time for her sake. It's not a feat you can just achieve otherwise. You or I can't simply stand on Main Street or Queen Street with a blow horn and shout, "Okay, everyone, back up. All streetcars just stay put for a half hour. I want to test your commitment."

Yet when the crunch comes, the people will give. Some people were a bit impatient. I heard the ever popular French benediction, *"Tabarnak"* uttered a few times by nearby motorists caught in the bottleneck. But they too accepted the situation and did not go over to the cops and say, "She's only one. We're dozens of vehicles and hundreds of people. Can you do something for us, too?"

And take the police officers themselves. They're out there on the street not using their sticks or their guns or their muscle (unless the tabarnaks start getting out of hand). Crime is now the last thing on their minds.

I imagine at the hospital there must have been a team of doctors, nurses, and other attendants who dealt with the lady's injuries. At the end of the day, she must have been the focus of the equivalent of a small town full of people. Even a television news team was there.

Joseph Stalin once said something like, "One person dying is a tragedy. A thousand people dying is a statistic."

What does this tell us about people? I never did like statistics.

ALL'S WELL AT THE WELL

The situation is even more dramatic whenever a child is involved. Every so often we hear of a child falling into a well, usually somewhere in Texas. Conventional rescue procedures fail and a small man is flown in who can be lowered into the well to scoop up the child. The event, which lasts a couple of days, is covered by all the major networks and news services. And at the end of it all, who pays for all this? Do the parents of the kid get a bill from the fire department? I doubt they get a rescue invoice which says something like, "for use of little man, 345 dollars." Money is never an issue. Although it always costs piles of dough, nobody ever pays. Or should I say nobody is any the poorer. It just happens. It happens.

MEDIC PLEASE

One thing has always puzzled me. I enjoy watching movies that have castle-storming sequences in them. I have seen oodles of these movies including *El Cid*, *The Vikings* and *Braveheart*. I usually root for the attackers. At least I am more sympathetic to their plight. Until they eventually break into the fortress, they have to put up with showers of flying rocks, arrows, and buckets of boiling sulphur being dumped on their heads. Until they hit pay dirt, they suffer the most casualties, probably by a ratio of twenty to one. That's why those Mexicans at the Alamo took those major hits though vastly outnumbering Davy Crocket and company.

Now I say casualties. We presume they all get killed. But what about the wounded? Surely some of the offenders don't kick the bucket while storming the castle; they just get singed by that hot sulphur. What happens to them? I have never seen one of these guys saying, "Help, I've fallen and I can't get up."

Surely they deserve as much attention as that lady on Rue Saint Denis.

It would make me feel a lot better if just once I would see a storming scene where the attackers bring along a team of medics who run over with a stretcher the minute one of their comrades suffers damage. Until then I'll always wonder what ever happens to these guys.

WE DO CARE

There are three things that under most circumstances complete strangers will do for one another. These are: render first aid, make change, and give directions.

SAVE WILLY

Although most of us don't really know a thing about first aid, we'll still give it our best shot. I remember when I was in first grade a group of us were swinging up and down on a mobile fire escape. It was a type of metallic swinging staircase which zig zags down the outside of a building with the last set remaining in the air held up by a counterweight in order to prevent kids from swinging on them.

One day my friend Willy injured his knee after falling off this neighborhood Magic Kingdom ride. As he sat there in the lane crying, his knee bruised and bleeding, waiting for the emergency people who had been summoned to the rescue, my mother ran out and brought him a bottle of 7-Up. He drank some of it while another lady held a wet rag against his knee.

My mother was quite proud of herself, indicating to all at every opportunity how she helped save Willy, how he lit up and beamed when she gave him that green bottle.

I know it may not have been textbook first aid. I don't think there is a St. John's Ambulance handbook around which reads, "Chapter 4, bloody knees, keep patient still, elevate leg, get him a 7-Up."

But I am sure it did help in some form or another. And I am certain Willy remembers the drink to this day, more than that wet rag.

DO YOU HAVE CHANGE FOR . . .

A twenty? A cute clerk at the bus station once responded by giving me back another twenty. A bit crisper maybe.

This is a ritual we all frequently go through both as a changer and a changee. This is one of the most frequently played out events indicating people's interdependence on one another. We'll approach total strangers to ask for change. And the changee will never run away upon hearing the proposition of changing a dollar into four quarters.

This is a different ritual of course from the panhandler asking you for some spare change. I always wondered about that one. I work hard for my money, and although I am far from greedy, I have not yet reached my monetary saturation point. I can't think of anyone who has. It's not like that graphic ten-foot-tall thermometer we see in charity-drive campaigns which indicates how much the fund has received to date in pledges on route to achieving their goal of three million dollars. I don't think most of us have that magic number which if achieved, all other monies coming into the kitty constitute spare change. Bill Gates certainly doesn't have one. And if he did it wouldn't be ten feet tall.

You see when you make change, the parties undergo a serious business venture. They each give value for value. The person with the dollar gets four quarters enabling him to make a phone call or use a vending machine. He's happy. The other guy gets rid of that loose change, replacing it with one note or if you live in my parts with a coin bearing the Queen's picture on it attesting to the fact the coin is worth those four quarters also bearing the Queen's picture. (Her Majesty certainly gets around. No way she has time for those shoplifters!)

Although both parties are even, each is now happier he or she accommodated the other. I have noticed some people take the ritual further. I once needed a single to take a city bus ride. I only had a five dollar bill. I stopped a scruffy-looking bearded man on the street and he had a single but not enough of them to make change. He told me to take the dollar bill. "It's okay," he said. "Maybe you'll just return the favor to another guy in a similar predicament one day. Or maybe we'll meet (pointing to the sky) up there eventually and you can repay me then."

We chatted further and he told me he was a philosophy lecturer at York University. I thanked him, but I really wanted to repay him. In Toronto. It was none of St. Peter's business.

He gave me his first name and I tracked him down and mailed him the dollar together with a thank-you note. He wrote back saying I really shouldn't have done it and he wished me well.

I have since forgotten his first name, and I imagine he has probably forgotten the entire incident. But the encounter left a lasting impression on me.

I have since emulated the man by giving or forgiving this extra ten percent or more to people who didn't have the exact change. Sometimes if the occasion permits I even gave them a business card after introducing myself. And you know what? So far I'm out about ten to fifteen dollars. Not one of them has ever looked me up, not even to ask for more money. Maybe they figure, "He's a lawyer, he doesn't need the buck."

Maybe I should get business cards calling myself a philosophy lecturer. I used to have a beard.

It doesn't matter really. I'm happy. If you ever see me on the street and you're stuck for change, I'm open for business. How's that for random acts of kindness?

DO YOU KNOW THE WAY TO . . .

Unless you're in some parts of New York City, most of us will readily go over to the closest person and ask for directions. As in the making change ritual, the party of the second part, call him the local, will usually feel honored to be of service. Either he'll give you what you seek, or he'll tell you he doesn't know or at worst, he'll give you the wrong directions accidentally. If that happens he'll still walk away proud of himself and feeling like he's been of service.

You on the other hand will feel good and secure initially until you realize after walking ten blocks that

John Avenue is ten blocks east of where the Good Samaritan mislead you. You have walked ten blocks west. Welcome to John Boulevard.

Which brings me to Boston. I visited that city when I was seventeen years old because I simply wanted to see it. I headed east to seek my adventures. I'd pace the downtown area with a large map in front of my face and whenever I stopped someone for directions, their first response was in a thick Kennedy accent, "You wolkin'?"

I had that happen to me so many times it drove me bananas.

Twenty-five years later I returned with my family, and we got a little bit lost, mostly as a result of the one-way streets that enable you to see your destination street. It's only one block away, but you are prevented from getting to it because you have to know the secret sequence of turns to reach it. If you don't crack the code to the maze, either you'll burn a tank of gas circling the downtown area or worse, you'll give up and end up in Providence Rhode Island.

I spotted a police cruiser stopped nearby, and I shouted to the officer from my car, "How do I get to Court Street?" (Which was about one block away). The officer was busy scribbling on a clipboard and without raising his eyes at me he said, "You Wolkin'?"

We spent the night in Providence.

LIFE IN PARIS

It is said Parisians are supposed to be rude to visitors. And everybody knows Parisians won't give you the time of day, including directions. Or rather they more than likely will give you misleading directions.

I had grown up with this perception of Parisians and it accompanied me when my train pulled into the Gard de Nord that evening back in 1968, marking my inaugural visit to Paris.

I had no idea where I was going as my eyes noticed the information kiosk. My pals had all warned me about this city of nasty people. It was with trepidation that I lined up at the kiosk with my two heavy pieces of luggage. I felt about as comfortable as the three little pigs asking the wolf for advice on architecture.

The line at the booth was a bit long and so I said to myself, "It figures. The kiosk people are probably stonewalling the tourists, not giving them anything." I decided I didn't need their misleading information anyway and I left the station.

It then occurred to me I did not know where I would be spending the night. I had the name of a small hotel near the Notre Dame church, but I hadn't booked anything. I would have called them, but I was sure they would have told me there was no vacancy even though the place was empty. Parisians are that way you know.

And so I walked a block or two outside the station with my luggage getting heavier by the moment, which consisted of lots of stuff purchased in the friendlier European countries. Among other things, I was carrying two kilos of Hojkes (pronounced hopkies) the Dutch coffee candies.

It was getting dark now and I was also hungry. Against my better judgment I pulled over to a sidewalk cafe. A waiter wearing a large white apron and

147

sporting a bicycle bar moustache came over to take my order. As he was smiling from ear to ear, I had no doubt the food in this place was either toxic or at best stale and rancid.

Hey, this was Paris! Jean Valjean got twenty years here for stealing a loaf of bread to feed his hungry family. I made sure I still had my money on me before ordering. After all, this was pickpocket city.

I returned the waiter's probably phony smile with a smile of my own, as I did not want to show contempt lest he attack me with a cleaver. I ordered a piece of baguette with jam and a cafe. I figured this order was safe. It was also inexpensive, at least on the menu. I of course, expected the usual Parisian hidden charges. The result of which, should I be unable to pay, would find me washing the dishes.

To my surprise, my order arrived quickly. Then again I was sure the guinea pigs were usually the first to be fed.

I squeezed the bread and it crunched perfectly. It was probably in the oven while I was on my train. But then again I knew there was a trick here. The waiter could have accidentally given me the bread he used for the locals. He forgot to give me the frozen stuff reserved for tourists.

The *cafe* tasted as good as it smelled. The waiter offered me a refill but I refused. His apparently generous offer was no doubt motivated by the fact the poison in the first cup had not yet started to take effect. He wasn't fooling me. This guy's grandfather probably catered Rasputin's last meal.

We started gabbing and inadvertently I blurted out I had no place to stay yet. I happen to mention the Hotel de la Tournelle in the Latin Quarter, and I expected him to laugh and say, "Don't bother. It's always booked."

Instead, he telephoned the hotel and booked me a room for the night.

I wonder what's in it for him? I thought. *Maybe it's a trap. After all if this were four thousand years ago, this city would probably be twinned with Sodom and Gomorrah. I'll get there and they'll take my luggage and throw me out. And then they'll toss my Hojkes into the Seine. No way Jose.*

Then again I figured the hotel was my pick. I decided to chance it. I paid my bill and was about to leave when the waiter asked, "Monsieur, don't you wish me to tell you how to get there?"

Ah huh, I thought. I knew it was near the St. Michel metro station. I thought I'd play along with the guy, listening to him direct me to Athens. I had his number.

He said, "You must take the metro to St. Michel." He then went on to tell me how to get to the nearby metro station. Before I could lift my bags, he said, "Allow me to help. He then carried one of my bags walking along with me for three blocks to the metro. At the station he shook my hand and wished me a pleasant stay in Paris.

I felt like Kevin Costner and the group of Indians during their first close encounter in *Dances With Wolves*.

I arrived at the hotel and things only improved from there. I had a great time.

I recently came across a lost French tourist wandering around Toronto's Union Station. I offered to assist with his bags and he looked at me very suspiciously, spurning my bid. I wonder what his pals told him about us.

IT IS A FAR BETTER THING

Hardly a day goes by where we don't hear of people sacrificing their own safety and interests to help others. Every time a firefighter enters a flaming building there is a good risk he may not come out alive. Why does he take this risk? For forty-five thousand dollars per year? I doubt it.

Unlike soldiers, firefighters have greater options on whether or not to take the risk. And there are still small communities here and there where there is no permanent fire department and where the local residents volunteer to run down to the small depot and man the equipment in the event of a fire. There is something that drives these people to throw risk to the wind. Which is why I felt sorry for the fire station in the Laurentian mountain village of Val Morin Quebec in the 1950s. You see, the village sported a handsome-looking station with an old pumper and a team of volunteers who would race thereto whenever Mr. Lesage, the nearby butcher, would sound the siren. In the event of a fire you called the butcher.

The station had a tall brick tower, a landmark of sorts, visible from afar. I used to spend my summers in the village and one summer when I returned, I noticed the tower was gone. So was the fire station for that matter. It had burnt down. True story.

I never did find out the full details. I imagine the locals wouldn't have boasted about the event. Maybe the butcher blew it. Who knows? I found out, however, that the volunteer force still remained intact and they were available for assignments if called upon in an emergency, albeit sans their fire station.

They eventually put a new pumper into a make-shift station in a small concrete garage. I imagine this one was fireproof. On the roof was a huge siren which went off by pushing a button a hundred yards or so away by you know who, Monsieur Lesage. Life went on.

I don't know about you but in the event of a fire I would have been a bit leery to call these guys. It would be like a teenager going to a dermatologist with acne.

But you have to give the volunteers credit. They were determined to serve and protect. They wouldn't inspire the creation of the movie *Towering Inferno*. But, nonetheless, they were ready to put it all on the line.

I, in fact, visited the town last summer and I was pleased as punch to notice the fire station was still standing. To my dying day, however, I shall wonder how that old fire station ever burnt down.

SYDNEY

In my book, the epitome of self-sacrifice was the act of Sydney Carton in Dickens' *Tale of Two Cities*. Sydney Carton, in an effort to make his condemned lookalike and the latter's fiancee happy, works his way into the cells of a Paris prison and with an assistant, conks out the look alike, and trades places with him, choosing to go to the guillotine in his place.

Before Madame Guillotine does her business, Sydney utters the immortal sentence, "It is a far better thing I do now than I have ever done before."

Now that's self-sacrifice. The ultimate. On top of everything he was an Englishman, getting caught up into the problems of the French Revolution. He was even a lawyer, a barrister. To all you skeptics about lawyers, put that into your pipe and smoke it!

Personally, I felt sorry for Sydney. I think he still should have tried to avoid his fate after switching places. Surely there is something he could have done. Maybe he could just have divulged the ruse before the end, telling everyone he was really English and casually joking about the switch. The French would obviously have realized he was not the condemned man. Perhaps they would have laughed the matter off and sent Sydney back on the next boat to England, admonishing him not to interfere in the ongoing reign of terror again.

You never know. Madame Defarge (no relation to the butcher in Val Morin) probably would not have been amused. But hey, it would have been a shot.

NEWTON'S OTHER LAW

Just as people are ready to give their all to complete strangers, the beast within us can readily surface, finding us clutching at our brothers' throats.

BEEP BEEP

The beast is often a passenger sitting close by when we drive a car. How do you feel when you get cut off by a dipsy-doodling vehicle? How do you like getting tailgated? What do you fell like doing to the motorist who shoots ahead of you in a shopping mall and grabs *your* parking spot? How do you enjoy sitting in your car at an intersection in the left turn lane when the traffic signal is red, behind the person who just sits there for a good three seconds after he gets a green left turn arrow? Exactly!

And what would happen if every vehicle came equipped with some James Bondian button you could press whenever the above-captioned annoys you and which would rid you of the culprits?

Let us assume even further there would be no repercussions from the law if you press such a button. How many people would do it? How many incidents do we read about per year of shootings on the Los Angeles freeways and other places in similar circumstances, where there are repercussions? Exactly!

This certain feeling does surge into all of us at one point or other, whereby the beast takes over the steering wheel. I'll bet dollars to donuts it happens and has happened to the best of us, including the likes of Gandhi and Dr. Leo Buscaglio. I just don't see Buscaglio driving into a mall and some sports car steals his parking spot and Buscaglio says, "I hope he enjoys this spot. Bless him. I will come out and give this person a hug."

Perhaps I should qualify that. Gandhi or Leo Buscaglio or the late Norman Vincent Peale may very well have had these sentiments, but not as an initial reaction. Firstly, I think the primitive instinct would have tried to surface and take over. Then, after these good people restrained it with their seatbelt, the love and understanding might have poured out. First . . . and then.

In my opinion, however, there is only one person who can consistently and successfully maintain this struggle with himself. You all know who that is: the reasonable man on the Clapham Street omnibus.

I'M FOIST

The beast is also not too far away wherever there is a line of people. In the cute one act play by Israel Horowitz entitled, *Line,* a group of people spend the entire play interacting while they stand for hours in a line waiting to see a baseball game. Although there are only a handful of people, and there is no doubt they'll each get in, they spend their time arguing and jostling for who's first.

How do you feel about the people standing in a movie queue after you find out tickets to what you want to see are sold out? How do you feel at a super-market when a person with twelve items lines up ahead of you at the express register which is limited to eight items? How do you feel when a person even with one item, shoots ahead of you? Exactly! The beast puts down the *National Enquirer* he or she is reading, and it takes over your shopping cart pronto.

But what happens if this person carrying just a stock of broccoli says, "Excuse me sir, all I have is this broccoli. May I get ahead of you?" Have you ever heard anyone say, "No"?

I haven't.

In this case you have the civilized strings playing in your mind. You are set to smile, be polite, make change, give directions, even volunteer to put out a fire if called upon.

Some of us might even sneak into Parisian dungeons to trade places with lookalike condemned prisoners. I don't think I would. But it's a thought.

I like to believe most of us operate at this level most of the time. But I sure am glad none of us have access to that button.

THE BALANCE

Getting back to those saints in that parking lot, the question is how long does it take to put that seatbelt around the beast? This varies form person to person and from situation to situation. And isn't this what it all comes down to?

The twentieth century has seen the end of the Wild West, where people who tick one another off for one small reason or other could arbitrarily have it out to the death, in a setting sanctioned by law.

And although the standards of living have drastically improved, we find wanton crimes of violence on the rise. The Attila the Huns and the Ivan the Terribles are all alive and well in their twentieth century reincarnations of Hitler and Stalin, *et al.*

The wanton violence bothers me. In the movie *Grand Canyon*, a mugger steps up to Steve Martin and asks for his watch at gunpoint. When Steve Martin hesitates and then offers him his sports car also, the mugger shoots him in the thigh, causing severe and permanent damage. Why didn't he just say "thank you" and take the car too?

Dr. Bernie Siegal, noted surgeon and author, known for his humanistic approach in dealing with patients, tells the story of a robber who demanded a reverend's wallet. The rev apparently handed the money over and said to the man something like, "Bless you. I know there is someone under that mask who could be loved."

155

In response the man returned the wallet and took off empty-handed. Many years later while the rev was giving a talk, the mugger showed up and reintroduced himself to the rev indicating that experience had turned his life around. It sort of reminds you of that part in *Les Miserables* when the bishop gives Jean Valjean, who had just stolen one of a pair of candlesticks, the second candlestick. This gesture turned Jean's life around too. And what a play followed!

Somehow we all have these strings in our brains that, when played, cause us to act with opulence and altruism. Similarly, we have a beast lurking within us. Unfortunately, it takes less effort to bring it to the fore.

I don't doubt that even the worst of people have good stuff waiting to be accessed. I am certain Al Capone, if asked for directions, would have readily told a tourist how to get to Chicago's Wrigley Field. He may even have given the guy a lift in his limo.

And let us recall how Hitler started out. As a starving artist. His application to join an art academy in Vienna was rejected, thereby making him available for other lines of work. What would have happened had he been accepted to the art academy? He would have probably succeeded as a painter. There would have been art exhibitions here and there featuring stuff by Picasso, Monet, and Hitler. I can just visualize an auction at Christie's of London peddling some of the paintings: "And here we have a fine oil by an Austrian artist who signs his painting as A. Hitler. It's called, 'A fruit bowl.' Notice the sharp hues. This young painter is going to go places."

Still others might say you can't keep a good man down. I imagine it's possible that if Adolf was successful as a painter, he could perhaps have become more ambitious than other painters. But then again we all could have lived with an artist who insisted on signing his paintings "Der Fuhrer." It's okay. Samuel Clemens signed his work "Mark Twain."

But you have to admit that at least the destiny of the world would have been altered drastically had Adolf been accepted at that art school and contented himself with painting fruit bowls or naked women.

There probably would never have been a World War II.

Where would all this have left Sir Winston Churchill? His finest hour then would have consisted of smoking a cigar and feeding the pigeons at Trafalgar Square. How about that for rain on your parade?

HAVE A HEART

In the Talmud there is a discussion among six distinguished scholars who ask the question, "What is the best quality to which a man should cling?"

One says, "A good eye," meaning generosity. Another says, "A good friend," meaning friendliness. Another one says, "justice," and so on. Rabbi Elazar ben Arach says, "A good heart."

His mentor Rabbi Yohanan ben Zakkai gives Rabbi Elazar the nod, saying that in his words, the words of the others are also included.

Presumably if someone has a good heart, this person will act with compassion, generosity, justice, and fairness. Presumably that person will be content with conquering a bit less than the entire world, financially, socially, athletically, or otherwise. Maybe this person would also grin and bear it and not fret and fume when someone jumps in line ahead of him. Just maybe the beast would be tamed to become a little puppy that surfaces occasionally to yelp rather than a raging pit bull that sits on our heads like the Cheshire Cat.

And how does one achieve a good heart? This is a moot question. One just has to know that it is good to have a good heart. We can then find our own ways to achieve this optimum temperament.

It would help if parents and teachers realize this and spread the word to the kids.

I recall reading a newspaper story about hockey hall of fame goalie Ken Dryden. He was engaged in a pressure cooker playoff game against the Boston Bruins. It seems one of the Boston goons charged in quickly and found himself accidentally falling over Dryden's leg. The all-star goalie apparently caught the Bruin player and said to him, "I'm sorry."

In a subsequent interview, the Bruin player indicated he was ready to start the customary fist fight with Dryden for deliberately tripping him, notwithstanding that Dryden at six-foot-six was a head and a half taller than him. He, however, mellowed instantly as he did not know how to react to this simple and rarely before seen gesture of courtesy.

It is of note that in another article years later there was a report about the goalie's father being involved in a charitable foundation he had engineered, whereby the dad supplied thousands of blankets and other equipment and goodies to impoverished children in third world countries.

Do you think some of this magnanimity was passed on to the big goalie? You don't have to be a sociologist to answer that one.

Don't get me wrong. It's quite possible the father of that Boston player was equally involved in community service. He may not have delivered all those blankets around the globe. But perhaps he was involved coaching minor hockey. It's just that he may have had a different theory on the absolute and critical importance of winning a hockey game.

WE ARE NOT AMUSED?

It amazes me how Queen Victoria lived well into her eighties if she was not amused. And why was she not amused? Maybe she was stressed out having to prosecute all those criminals for over sixty years. Who knows?

The twentieth century started off with Her Majesty Queen Victoria leaving. And with the Wright brothers shortly thereafter doing what the birds did, at Kitty Hawk. We all really developed from there.

Leacock said, "The world's humor, in its best and greatest sense, is perhaps the highest product of our civilization."

I believe it would help if we would all see a distinction between being serious and being responsible. Instead of being serious, we would marry responsibility to humor. This perspective just might do something to our one-on-one relations.

There is a joke I like. Three local and nearby butcher stores sell sausages. (None of the stores are owned by Monsieur Lesage.) They compete fiercely. One advertises, "Best sausages in town." The next day the second one puts out an ad, "Best sausages in the world." The third one not to be outdone, puts out a sign, "Best sausages in the neighborhood."

Isn't that where it really all has to start?

THE END

GIVE THE GIFT OF
BIRTH, DEATH AND OTHER TRIVIALITIES
TO YOUR FRIENDS AND COLLEAGUES

CHECK YOUR LEADING BOOKSTORE OR ORDER HERE

❑ **YES**, I want ___ copies of *Birth, Death and Other Trivialities* at $12.95 U.S. and $14.95 Canada each, plus $3 shipping per book (California residents please add $1.07 state sales tax per book). Canadian orders must be accompanied by a postal money order in U.S. funds. Allow 15 days for delivery.

❑ **YES**, I am interested in having Marcel Strigberger speak or give a seminar to my company, association, school, or organization. Please send information.

My check or money order for $____ is enclosed.

Please charge my ❑ Visa ❑ MasterCard

Name _____

Organization _____

Phone _____

Address _____

City/State/Zip _____

Card # _____

Exp. Date_____ Signature _____

Please make your check payable and return to:
Three Beans Press
115 Reflections Dr., #15
San Ramon, CA 94583

Call your credit card order to: (800) 723-5718
Fax: (416) 971-9092